# Success Stories

**Canadian Cataloguing in Publication Data:**

Davie, Michael B.
Success Stories: Business Achievement
in Greater Hamilton & Beyond

Includes index.
ISBN 1-895208-03-3

1. Business enterprises - Ontario - Hamilton. 2. Business enterprises - Ontario - Niagara Peninsula. 3. Businessmen - Ontario - Hamilton. 4. Businessmen - Ontario - Niagara Peninsula. 5. Success in business - Ontario - Hamilton. 6. Success in business - Ontario - Niagara Peninsula. I. Ruberto, Bruno. II. Title.

HF3230.H34D38 1997   338.7'09713'52   C97-931938-2

COPYRIGHT 1997
by BRaSH Publishing Incorporated & Michael B. Davie
All Rights Reserved

Published 1997

Printed in Canada by Friesens Corporation
First Edition

▲
*With a population of more than 320,000, The City of Hamilton is the heart of the Golden Horseshoe, a vast economic region that stretches all the way from Niagara Falls to Oakville.*
– PHOTO BY DAVID GRUGGEN

**BRaSH Publishing Incorporated**
Hamilton, Ont., Canada

## About The Author

Award-winning author Michael B. Davie was born Nov. 8, 1954 in Hamilton, Ontario. An early interest in writing led him to contribute his talents to a number of obscure publications while still in his teens in the late 1960s through early 1970s.

By the mid-1970s, Davie's professional career was under way as Editor of The Phoenix serving Mohawk College where he earned a Broadcast Journalism diploma.

He also holds a Niagara College print journalism diploma and degrees in Political Science from McMaster University where he was named to the Deans' Honour List and won the Political Science Prize for outstanding academic achievement.

After leaving The Phoenix, Davie served two years as regional news editor for one of Ontario's largest chains of community newspapers. He went on to work as a journalist, columnist and editor for the daily Welland Tribune.

Davie returned to the Steel City in 1980 to accept a position as a senior journalist with The Hamilton Spectator where he covered an array of assignments, including sensational courtroom trials, Queen's Park and a decade of business and financial issues. His work has appeared in many other Canadian and U.S. periodicals and he continues to write on steel trade for international magazines.

After nearly 17 years with The Spectator, Davie left the daily newspaper to found his own writing services company. The author of Success Stories also co-authored Hamilton: It's Happening, with Sherry Sleightholm.

Throughout the course of a long and distinguished career, Davie has won dozens of writing awards including several Western Ontario Newspapers Awards. His most recent WONA Business Writing Award was in April 1997. The same month, he was presented with a national Lifetime Achievement Award for journalism at ceremonies in Vancouver.

He resides in Ancaster with his wife Philippa and their children, Donovan, Sarah and Ryan.

## Acknowledgements

Writing this book has been a inspiring journey into the lives of dynamic, successful individuals.

I've enjoyed an almost magical, creative experience in which a simple idea and many long hours of hard work ultimately resulted in a thought-provoking book which had never existed before.

This rewarding and lasting achievement would not have been possible without the full co-operation, support and encouragement of the featured business leaders and economic experts. They lend substantial content and substance to this 53,420-word book.

Also essential to the creation of this fine book is Bruno Ruberto, president of BRaSH Publishing, who crafted the effective presentation of Success Stories. Bruno's expertise in page design, layout and editorial organization provided Success Stories with its eye-catching appeal. His exhaustive behind-the-scenes production and managerial efforts were vital in bringing this book from conception to finished product.

I'd also like to thank David Gruggen for giving Success Stories its visual impact with his stunning photography that illuminates and illustrates my narrative.

Finally, my thanks and love to my wife Philippa for her unwavering support towards making my career transition – and this book – truly successful endeavours.

*– Michael B. Davie*

# A Message From

On behalf of Hamilton-Wentworth region I'd like to commend Success Stories, author Michael B. Davie and BRaSH Publishing for focusing some long overdue attention on the many successful individuals and businesses driving our region's economy.

As I write this, Hamilton-Wentworth's population is about 470,000 people and is steadily closing in on the half-a-million population mark. Within the 112,136 hectares of space that belong to our region, you can find a stunning degree of diversity unmatched anywhere else.

You can enjoy both city and country life in Stoney Creek, a community steeped in history which also remains a great place to savour soft fruits and great wine.

Or you can take in the bustling small-town spirit of Dundas, our picturesque valley town.

Of course you won't want to miss historic Ancaster and its wealth of conservation lands. Our oldest community, it consistently ranks as one of Canada's wealthiest centres.

Flamborough boasts an interesting mix of agriculture and high-tech industries while Glanbrook is home to Hamilton International Airport, a vital part of our region's transportation network and one of our biggest success stories.

At the heart of it all is Hamilton itself, a major Canadian city, an industrial giant, a centre of higher learning, a hotbed for health sciences and an environmental role model for the entire world.

We're the steel-making capital of Canada, a major port and a recreational centre. We truly have it all.

Success Stories puts a welcome spotlight on some of the influential players who have helped shape, and continue to shape, our collective destiny.

*– Terry Cooke,*
*Regional Chairman,*
*Hamilton-Wentworth Region*

As the Mayor of Hamilton, it gives me great pleasure to welcome the arrival of this exceptional book chronicling the success stories of our city and some of its prominent individuals and companies.

Success Stories recognizes the City of Hamilton's historic and ongoing role as the hub of an economic region that extends well beyond our municipal borders. Hamilton forms the core of an international economic sphere that encompasses 120 million people within a 500-mile radius. That's a huge market all within a day's drive of our city.

Success Stories also details the ways in which our economy has diversified while retaining and revitalizing our industrial base. Hamilton remains Canada's Steel City, a major commercial centre, the home of high-tech companies, and a centre for health sciences and higher leaning.

Compared with other major centres, Hamilton boasts an impressive supply of relatively inexpensive real estate coupled with a highly skilled workforce and a City Hall that welcomes and encourages new business and investment.

All the right ingredients are here for business success – and I hereby extend warmest greetings and an open invitation to outside businesses to consider our city's central location when developing expansion plans.

Success Stories author Michael B. Davie has continued the enthusiastic momentum he helped create as co-author of the book Hamilton – It's Happening, celebrating our city's sesquicentennial.

Hamilton has much to offer – and I never tire of praising this remarkable city. In this enjoyable role, I'm joined by Success Stories which presents an honest, positive appraisal of our ambitious city and its many strengths.

*– Robert M. Morrow,*
*Mayor,*
*The City of Hamilton*

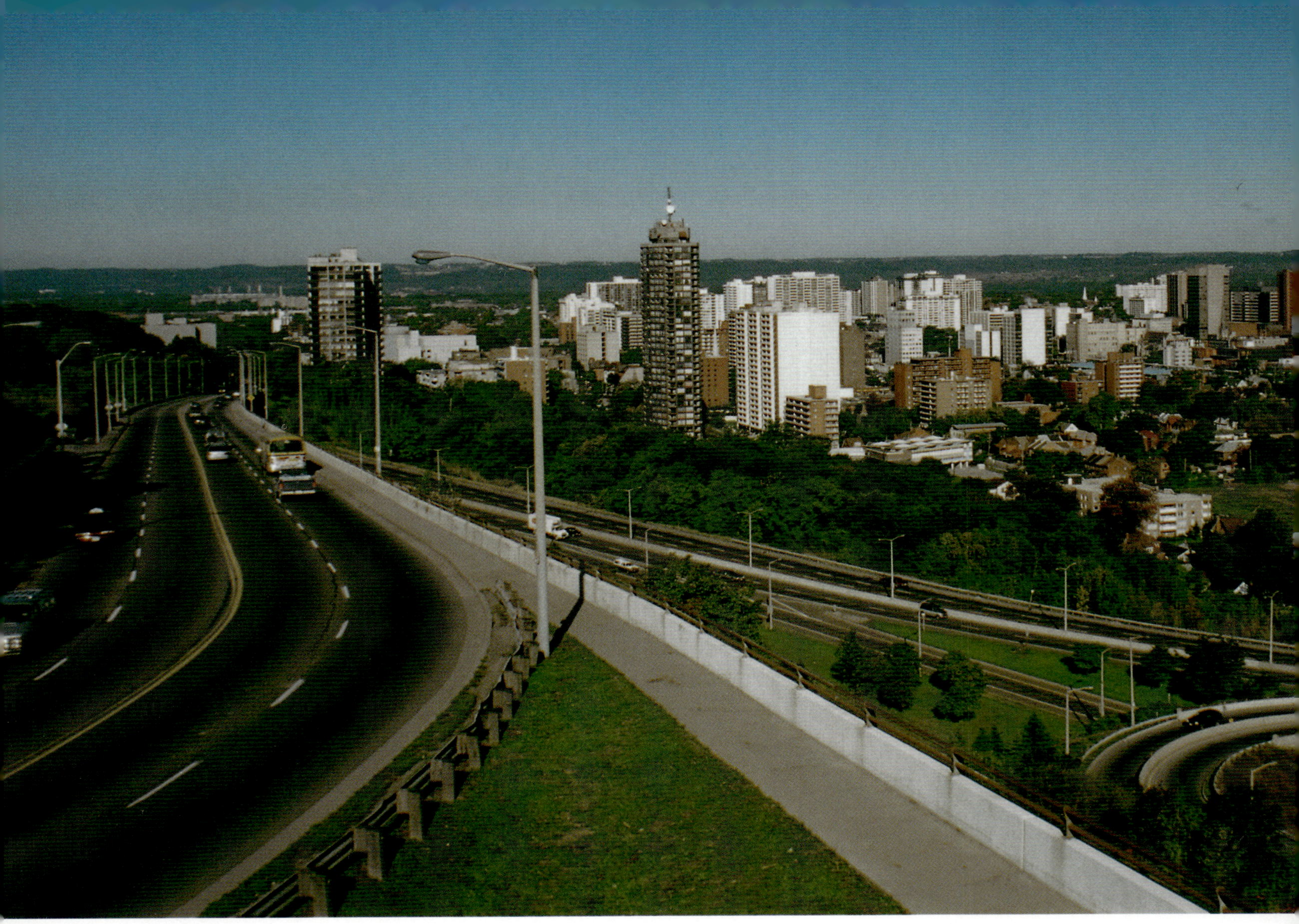

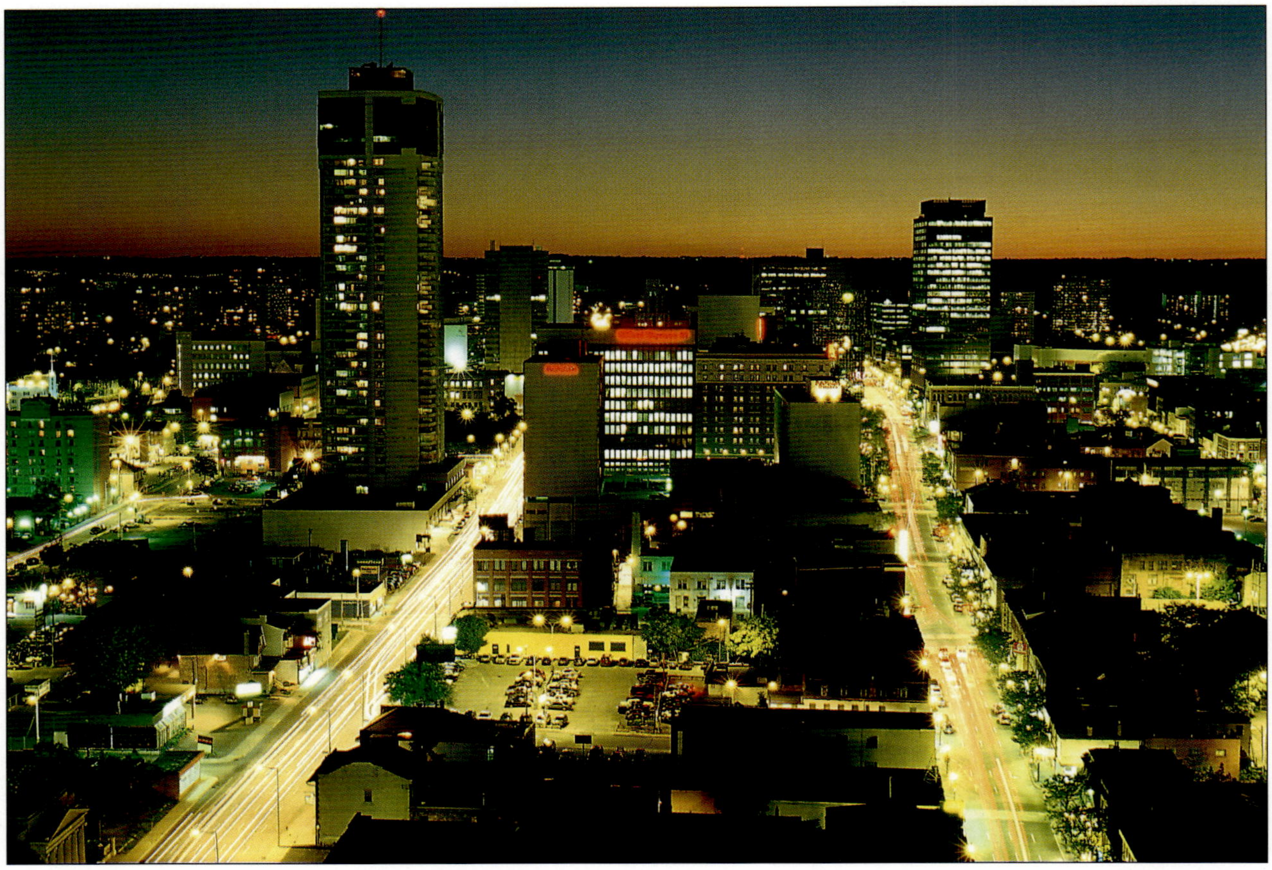

# Contents

**CHAPTER 1**
*Gateway To Prosperity*

**CHAPTER 2**
*The Hub Of The Horseshoe*

**CHAPTER 3**
*Industry & Transportation*

**CHAPTER 4**
*Financial Advisors*

**CHAPTER 5**
*The Entrepreneurs*

**CHAPTER 6**
*Media Managers*

**CHAPTER 7**
*Service Providers*

**CHAPTER 8**
*On The Homefront*

**CHAPTER 9**
*A Look Ahead*

▲
Major transportation arteries wind through the heart of Hamilton. The city's roadways, along with a modern airport and industrial harbour, facilitate the movement of goods and services throughout the greater economic region.
– PHOTO BY DENNIS MCGREAL

◄
A new day dawns on Hamilton's commercial core. With fresh signs of vitality, the downtown is awakening to a renewed spirit of optimism.
– PHOTO BY DENNIS MCGREAL

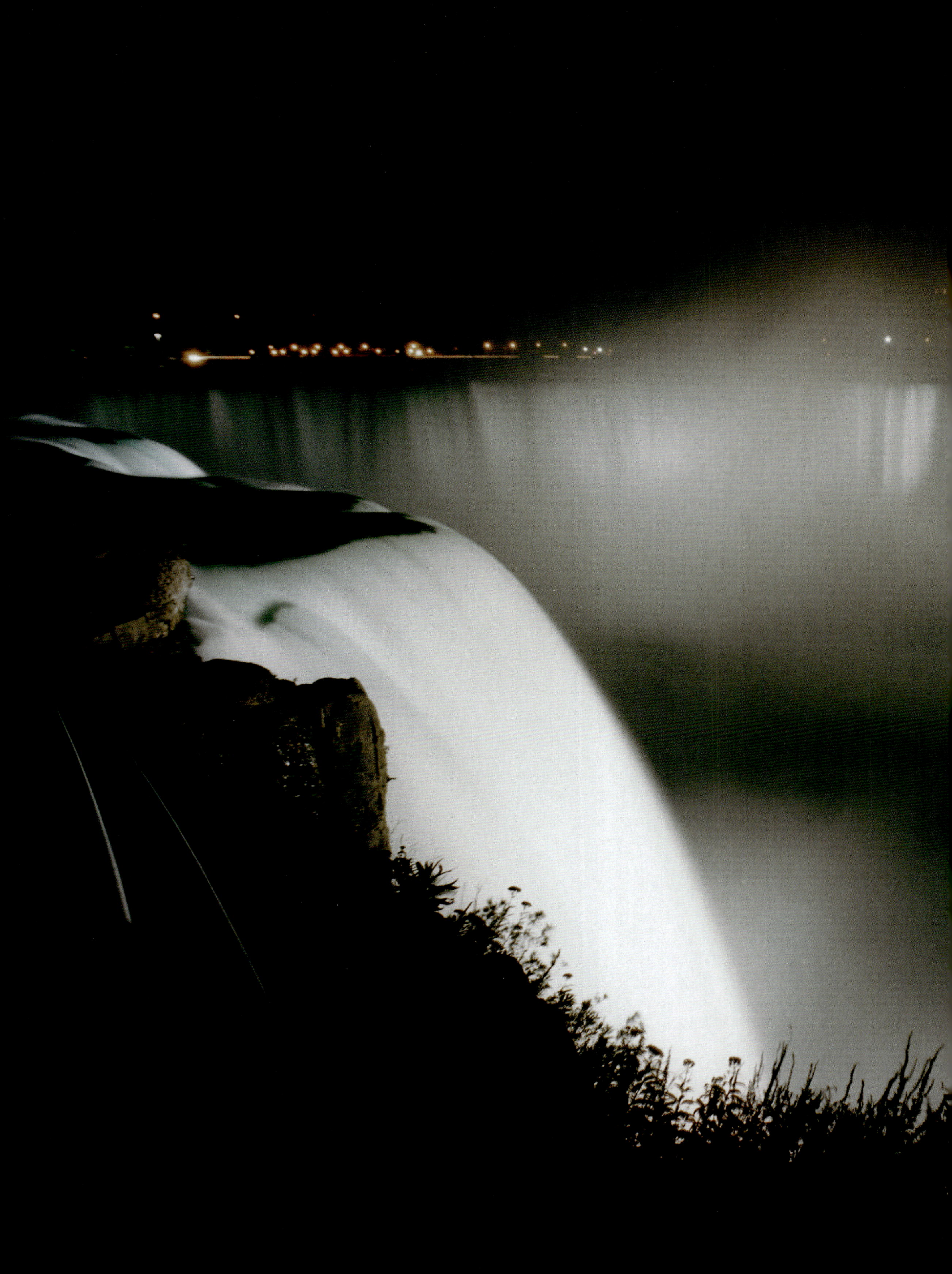

# Preface

Shrouded in mist, obscured by the roaring, plunging waters of Niagara Falls, lies an unseen, compelling gateway to a vast, prosperous economic region.

Stretching westward from the Niagara River, bending around Lake Ontario, this region extends eastward on the north side of the lake, taking in much of Halton region before blurring into the Toronto sprawl.

Encompassing the Golden Horseshoe outside of Toronto and often overshadowed by the Toronto metropolis, this lesser known, distinctive economic region is home to a remarkably diverse, interdependent economy.

Boasting an array of physical and commercial attractions, this economic region sustains more than 1 million Canadians amid lush agricultural lands, urban centres, heavy industry, commerce and leading high-tech companies.

At the hub – and the heart – of this expansive community is Greater Hamilton with its Steel City core rising confidently from the southwestern head of Lake Ontario.

Nightfall. And the Ambitious City is a sea of glowing lights banked by its harbour and the forest-fringed waters of Cootes' Paradise to the west.

Many first-time visitors to Hamilton are often pleasantly surprised at just how green it is. The city's urban centre appears as an island, all but surrounded by water to the north, forested conservation and recreation lands to the west, farmland to the south and east.

The city itself is home to an array of parks and green spaces. Yes, Hamilton is the unrivalled steel-making capital of Canada. But it's an industrial city which has learned to accommodate industry needs with the population's realized demands for a high quality of life.

Rest assured, steel remains an integral, enduring, defining element shaping Hamilton's identity and destiny as the resilient core of the nation's industrial heartland. Stelco Inc. and Dofasco Inc. are respectively the nation's two largest steelmakers and the city's two biggest individual employers.

Together they directly provide some 14,000 jobs. Hamilton will always proudly call itself Canada's Steel City. Yet there is so much more to Greater Hamilton and beyond than heavy industry.

Success Stories is a business book intent on challenging some of the stereotypes associated with one of the most vibrant economic regions in all of Canada. The focus of this book is on peeling back some of the layers of obscurity that mask the intriguing success stories found in this region.

I'll introduce you to some remarkable, inspiring entrepreneurs, provide a behind-the-scenes look at some dynamic, unusual companies – and shed some light on the potent business strategies employed by billionaire businessman Michael DeGroote, our most striking example of a local man who made it big and continues to conquer new horizons.

No offence, Toronto, but we have some great success stories of our own – and I'm here to tell you about some of them.

In fact, our economic region is literally filled with interesting, intriguing success stories.

This volume of Success Stories will examine just a few of them.

*– Michael B. Davie.*

◀

*The awe-inspiring majesty of Niagara Falls forms a dramatic entrance to the beckoning lights of the Honeymoon Capital and the many cities beyond.*
*– PHOTO BY DAVID GRUGGEN*

– PHOTO BY DAVID GRUGGEN

# CHAPTER 1

# *Gateway To Prosperity*

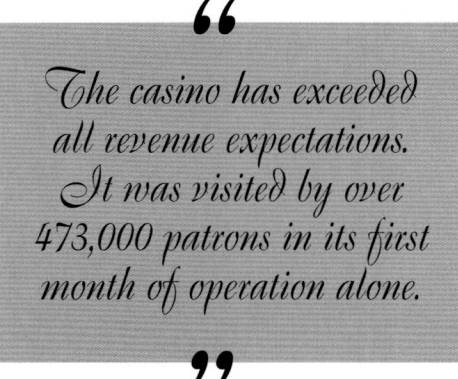

# Gateway To Prosperity

You couldn't invent a more dramatic entrance to the Golden Horseshoe and our vast economic region than Niagara Falls, a churning, thundering, plunging cascade of water and mist.

The Niagara River flows deceptively slowly, northward from Lake Erie, then suddenly assumes a determined sense of urgency as it approaches The Falls. The river now takes on a forceful life of its own, rushing relentlessly towards the precipice, then plummeting in a liquid roar, smashing into Lake Ontario below.

This terrifyingly beautiful spectacle of Niagara Falls, one of the Seven Wonders of the World, has inspired writers and dare devils, artists and lovers.

And it's inspired business people. Witness the gleaming new casino, the many hotels and restaurants, the Lundy's Lane strip of tourist attractions, the Skylon Tower, Marineland and the sprawling city of Niagara Falls.

This intensive commercialization and urbanization begins just west of the Niagara River and continues westward, interrupted sporadically by farmland, throughout the Niagara Region.

In the city of Niagara Falls, Casino Niagara has exceeded all revenue expectations. Opened on December 9, 1996, the casino was visited by over 473,000 patrons in its first month of operation alone.

During this initial month, these patrons spent $28.7 million, according to economic development highlights released by the Niagara Economic and Tourism Corporation.

The following month, January, 1997, Casino Niagara raked in $33.6 million, making it Ontario's most profitable casino.

In its first few months of operation, Casino Niagara averaged some 20,600 visitors each day – fully 25 per cent more than the 16,000 anticipated when this impressive landmark opened.

By mid-February, 1997, Casino Niagara had attracted about 1 million visitors and some $65 million in revenue.

The casino is another attraction in a city rich with attractions.

Although the warmer months of the year are the biggest tourist draw, the annual Winter Festival of Lights attracts over 1 million visitors annually. During the warmer months, visitors can view the awe-inspiring majesty of The Falls from the newest member of the Maid of the Mist fleet, the Maid of the Mist VII which carries 600 passengers at a time across the churning waters below this world-famous attraction.

The Niagara Falls City Centre commercial complex has brought 525 office workers into the city's downtown core. Factor Forms Niagara Ltd. has doubled the size of its Niagara Falls site and increased its workforce to 60 people.

These developments come as poignant reminders that there is more to business in Niagara than tourism.

Indeed, business investment seems to be growing on a daily basis in the city of Niagara Falls, home to 77,400 people – and a total of 14 million annual visitors.

And, there are other signs of growth and prosperity in Niagara, a regional municipality containing some 410,000 people in 12 municipalities ranging in size from small rural communities to the City of St. Catharines, an urban centre of 133,000 people.

Nestled between Lake Ontario and Lake Erie, just west of the Niagara River, the Niagara region is joined only by British Columbia's Okanogan Valley as one of Canada's very few region's capable of growing soft fruits.

The Niagara region is, in fact, a major centre for soft fruit of all types, particularly grapes which support the region's impressive, world-renowned wine industry.

Niagara's climate and geography allow it to produce world-class Riesling, Chardonnay and Pinot Noir grape varieties for premium wines meeting VQA (Vintners Quality Alliance) standards. All told, the Niagara region accounts for 80 per cent of Ontario's $215 million wine industry.

Fully two-thirds of Ontario's tender fruit growing lands are in Niagara region.

Grape production alone accounts for 15,000 acres of growing lands.

Niagara also boasts almost 1 million square feet of greenhouse space and the region's various greenhouses together employ over 2,000 people.

With a land mass of 1,800 square kilometres, Niagara region borders the United States. And, the region's four international crossings account for nearly 40 per cent of all international crossings between Canada and the United States. In 1995 alone, over 6.4 million same-day trips were recorded between Niagara and New York State, a 6.2 per cent increase over 1994.

> "The casino has exceeded all revenue expectations. It was visited by over 473,000 patrons in its first month of operation alone."

Niagara also features superb highway access with the Queen Elizabeth Way and a number of secondary highways running through its land mass.

Although Niagara's unemployment rate tends to be higher than nearby Hamilton's rate, it still boasts one of the nation's lower unemployment rates. The region has a largely skilled labour force of more than 152,000 people. The government sector – including school boards, hospitals and local municipal governments – accounts for over 20,000 jobs.

There are approximately 13,000 businesses in Niagara region and 42 per cent of the region's products are exported, primarily to the U.S. Major employers include General Motors of Canada, employing 5,200 people; TRW – Canada Ltd., employing 1,300; Atlas Specialty Steels, employing 1,100; plus Dana Canada Inc. and John Deere Ltd., which each employ about 1,000.

Other major employers include the region's media, consisting of daily newspapers St. Catharines Standard, Welland Tribune and Niagara Falls Review; plus numerous weekly newspapers, radio stations and cable television services.

The Niagara region is also a centre of higher learning, housing Brock University and Niagara College.

Success Stories

# Gateway To Prosperity

*Casino Niagara is another bright light in the heart of Niagara Falls. By mid-February, 1997, the casino had hosted 1 million visitors.*
– PHOTO BY DAVID GRUGGEN

The region is known for its parks, historic sites and stunning scenery. Evidence of growth is everywhere in this region.

Not far from the city of Niagara Falls, lies the city of Thorold, population 18,600 people, where Enviro-Ganics Ecological Systems Inc. has announced plans for a $2.3 million greenhouse operation providing 20 jobs.

Fort Erie has been named as one of Ontario's charity casino sites. The border town is also winning big with an expansion by Fleet Industries Ltd. which signed an 11-year contract worth over $200 million to produce wing components for the McDonnell Douglas MD-95 commercial aircraft for Hyundai Space and Aircraft Co. of South Korea.

The Fort Erie Race Track, one of the most beautiful tracks in Ontario, is being transformed into a major entertainment centre in this quaint community of 28,300 people.

Welland's Niagara College campus is adding a $5 million student residence to house 231 students. The city of Welland's population grew 11 per cent from 1986 to a total of 50,000 people in 1996. Welland is famous for its busy canal system and the city is Ontario's second steel city.

On the outskirts of Welland lies the picturesque, leafy town of Pelham. Primarily a residential centre with a bustling commercial strip, Pelham's population grew about 18 per cent in the 10-year period beginning in 1985 to reach 14,300 people in 1996.

With its main roadways sheltered by canopies of tree branches, Pelham is among the most pleasant places to live in Canada. It's home to many wealthy families.

Rural, farming-based communities are found in nearby Wainfleet, West Lincoln, Lincoln and Grimsby municipalities. Of these, Grimsby, bordering Hamilton-Wentworth region, is the largest of Niagara's rural communities and is home to 20,000 residents. These rural communities lend the region much of its rustic, agricultural charm and slow-paced quality of life.

The Shaker Cruise Lines service is now bringing tourists from Queens Quay West on Toronto's harbourfront to Port Dalhousie in Niagara. Some 300 tourists make each one-hour trip aboard Shaker's Lake Runner, adding significantly to the influx of tourists into the region.

Niagara's bustling city of Port Colborne, with a population of 19,000, is the first municipality in Ontario to own a shortline railway. The Port Colborne Harbour Rail Line began operations in June 1997.

*Success Stories*

# Gateway To Prosperity

▲ The Shaw Cafe & Wine Bar is the perfect setting for tourists to enjoy a fine meal during their visit to the scenic community of Niagara-on-the-Lake.
– PHOTO BY DAVID GRUGGEN

◄ A striking statue of playwright George Bernard Shaw, by Ancaster sculptor Elizabeth Holbrook, forms a focal point in Niagara-on-the-Lake.
– PHOTO BY DAVID GRUGGEN

*Success* 14 *Stories*

# Gateway To Prosperity

Known as the Garden City for its flower-filled boulevards and picturesque streets, St. Catharines is the region's largest city with 133,000 people.

It's also a major industrial centre and service centre, home to GM Canada and numerous automotive-related industries.

And business is booming in the Garden City. St. Catharines' General Motors plant has landed a work order guaranteeing 100 jobs at its components plant. Several new restaurants opened in the Garden City during 1997, creating hundreds of jobs.

Voice Recovery Services, a high-tech firm brought 600 jobs to St. Catharines in the spring of 1997 while the city's Port Weller Dry Docks landed a multi-million-dollar destroyer refit contract creating 200 jobs. And, an expansion of the Ramada Parkway Inn in St. Catharines created an additional 50 jobs.

Niagara-on-the-Lake, long-known as Canada's prettiest town, is establishing a new village community of 400 homes on 200 acres on the edge of town.

This development is to architecturally blend in with Niagara-on-the-Lake's historic and picturesque town centre. The community was home to 13,200 people in 1996 – and its beauty and serenity are attracting many new residents every year.

In other developments, Niagara-on-the-Lake's elegant Queen's Landing Hotel has undergone major renovations and expansions, nearly doubling the number of seats in its elegant Tiara restaurant to 220. Queen's Landing's enlarged hotel ballroom can now accommodate 320 people, allowing the hotel to attract more weddings, receptions, conventions and special functions.

"Elegant stained-glass ceilings, jade-textured walls and alabaster tiles create an elegance which will give the hotel the best advertising money can buy – word of mouth," says Nancy Bailey Brazeau, director of sales and marketing for the hotel.

"Drawing more business executives with money to spend at local shops will benefit the town overall," adds Bailey Brazeau.

This Queen's Landing Hotel and several other Niagara-on-the-Lake landmark inns are owned by businesswoman Si Wai Lai, who has invested many millions of dollars in the community. In addition to restoring and beautifying a number of historic inns, she commissioned the striking statue of playwright George Bernard Shaw, created by Ancaster sculptor Elizabeth Holbrook, which now forms a focal point in this scenic community.

Niagara-on-the-Lake attracts some 3 million visitors each year, making it the region's top tourist draw after Niagara Falls.

Further west lies the municipality of Lincoln, a rural collection of communities with a total population of almost 20,000 in 1996.

Only 10 years earlier, Lincoln's population was less than 14,400 people. Lincoln's 10-year growth rate of 36.2 per cent is by far the highest in Niagara region. It's growing twice as fast as closest rival, Pelham – which grows at a rate of about 18 per cent each decade. Most Niagara municipalities have been growing at considerably slower rates than either of these municipalities.

Driving Lincoln's population growth, in part, is its scenic setting, flanked by Lake Ontario and the Niagara Escarpment. Add in a temperate climate, rolling hills and interesting little communities such as Vineland, and you have a municipality where a growing number of people want to live.

This pressure for increased urbanization is at odds with efforts to preserve Lincoln's traditional role as an agricultural centre.

And the urbanization pressures are considerable. In the spring of 1997, the Township of Lincoln had the largest increase in building permit values of the 12 Niagara communities. Permit values jumped 378 per cent to $9.9 million from $2 million, mainly due to new housing permits.

Countering this urbanization trend is Niagara Land Company, a partnership which is developing disused and under-used agricultural lands into thriving vineyards.

Although up against a formidable foe in urbanization, it's hoped that this company will not be alone in trying to preserve one of our nation's few, soft fruit-growing lands.

A world-class culinary centre and winery are also planned by the NLC partnership, which consists of Vineland Estates Winery owner-proprietor John Howard, Vineland Estates founder Hermann Weis, London businessman Dieter Jahnke and Hamilton lawyer Paul Mazza.

> *Niagara-on-the-Lake attracts some 3 million visitors each year, making it the region's top tourist draw after Niagara Falls.*

Nearby the NLC properties at Vineland, Ontario, is John Howard's 14-room, chateau-style home – complete with turrets and nicknamed Castle Howard. This serenely beautiful retreat is known for its bold decorating touches, including his daughter Erin's showpiece, round-walled, tower bedroom boasting famed, skater-artist Toller Cranston's wall-to-wall fantasy artistry. The walls match Erin's bed, also painted by Cranston, which features a twisting jungle of painted vines and flowers.

Vineland Estates – an entirely separate entity from NLC – was acquired by Howard in 1992 from Weis, the winery's founder and a 16th generation winemaker from Germany's Mosel Valley.

"I didn't create this," Howard insists on pointing out. "I'm just a steward who has the responsibility of continuing the high standards set by the Weis family."

Yet, this 'steward' has done much to make Vineland Estates a success. He's restored the estate's carriage house into a banquet room and added a superb patio restaurant to this property, known for its rolling vineyards and award-winning wines.

A genuinely thoughtful and gracious host, Howard's unassuming manner and insistence on giving credit to others, have made this creative and astute businessman a fascinating character study of success. Howard and Vineland Estates are featured in a thought-provoking profile in the Entrepreneurs chapter of this book. Meanwhile, the NLC partnership's accomplishments also receive profile treatment, next.

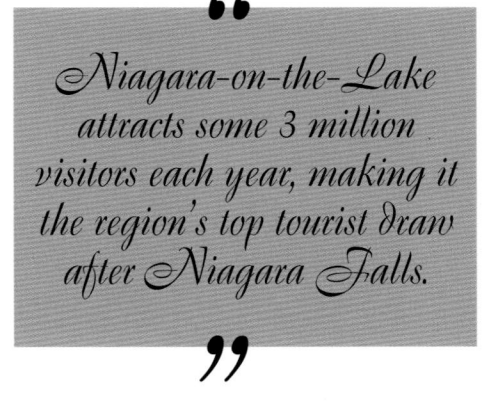

*The Vineland Estates vineyards produce world-class grapes which support Niagara region's impressive wine industry.*
– PHOTO BY DAVID GRUGGEN

Success Stories

# Niagara Land Company

Vintage years lie ahead for Niagara Land Company, a little-known firm which is shaping the destiny of the regional wine industry.

Better known are NLC's four partners, including company president John Howard, who is also owner of an entirely separate business, the Vineland Estates winery, vineyards and restaurant.

Remaining partners include Hamilton lawyer Paul Mazza, London, Ontario businessman Dieter Jahnke and Hermann Weis, the former owner of Vineland Estates who has a family tradition of winemaking in Germany's Mosel Valley going back 16 generations.

It's a dynamic partnership drawing on impressive degrees of business acumen and winemaking experience. Howard is clearly pleased, both with the NLC team, and with its bold expansion plans for Niagara's wine industry. "We're really excited about this," he exclaims.

There's good reason for excitement.

The NLC partners are currently involved in building a major wine business – and creating over 100 jobs.

With an initial investment of $8 million, NLC has acquired two major properties offering a combined total of more than 220 acres at Vineland, a community situated about midway between Hamilton and St. Catharines.

The acquired lands include a building that will be converted into a winery. NLC hopes to produce a million bottles of wine annually by the year 2000.

"We've acquired world-class plants from Europe to produce world-class wines we can export to world-class markets," says Howard, who expects growing domestic and export demand will easily consume NLC's annual production.

Of the two land acquisitions, NLC first acquired, in 1994, a 90-acre site largely consisting of farmland that had fallen into disuse. This property is opposite Howard's castle-like home on Tintern Road. The property has been restored to agricultural use through the planting of some 90,000 vinifera grape plants.

In 1996, NLC acquired its second key property, known as Bo-Teek Farms, a 128-acre site bordering Highway 8 to the north, giving it a prominent location on the Ontario Wine Route. This site underwent the planting of 40,000 vinifera grape plants in 1997. The planting of another 60,000 plants is planned for 1998.

At the Bo-Teek site, the creation of another winery is planned, using an existing circular building, once used for equestrian purposes, as the winery's nucleus.

Plans for the Bo-Teek site also include the proposed New World Culinary Centre, a $12 million wining, dining and educational facility. Here, some of Europe's and the Pacific Rim's finest chefs will teach the art of cuisine – either in person or on screens via satellite – using local produce grown year-round in a massive greenhouse to be built on-site.

> "We've acquired world-class plants from Europe to produce world-class wines we can export to world-class markets."

Howard is openly enthusiastic about the proposed centre, which he hopes to have operating by the grape harvest of 1998. However, the approvals which are needed – from the Niagara Escarpment Commission and Ontario Ministry of Natural Resources – could add a year or more to this timeframe.

"The centre will promote an awareness of the unique agricultural character of the Niagara region and the tremendous potential we have in both agriculture and tourism," Howard says proudly.

Howard notes that the proposal would also mean the preservation of agricultural land use at the site and beyond. The centre itself would also create a market for local farm produce, helping to resist urbanization pressure throughout Niagara.

Clearly, the centre will revolutionize the Niagara – and by extension, Canadian – wine industry, schooling future generations of vintners and chefs in the art of matching superb local wines to fresh, locally grown foods. Directly employing at least 50 people, the proposed centre would promote both the wine industry and Ontario agriculture as a whole.

The three-storey centre is to feature a 50-seat amphitheatre for wine and food education. This huge lecture theatre will back onto a massive, three-storey, two-acre greenhouse where native-to-Ontario herbs, legumes and spices will be grown year-round. Also featured in this self-contained community are 50 guest house units and an Old World wine cellar with dining facilities for 120 people, amid oak casks and barrels.

In addition to the finest European and Pacific Rim chefs, the centre will also feature the expertise of a superb local chef, Mark Picone, director of the centre, whose culinary magic is already familiar to patrons of Vineland Estates where he serves as executive chef.

Picone is to conduct recipe/cooking/dinner demonstrations at the centre on Cherry Avenue, which is also not far from Howard's Tintern Road home.

All four NLC partners have received commendations from federal Agriculture minister Ralph Goodale in recognition of their "substantive investment in leading edge viticultural technology," which includes the successful transplanting of German Riesling vinifera in Vineland.

"I am convinced," Goodale states, "that your adherence to responsible land use management, combined with your initiative, will further enhance the rejuvenation of the vineyards of the Niagara region."

Goodale singles out Weis for making "an outstanding contribution to the Canadian wine industry."

After founding Vineland Estates in 1983 and building it into a successful winery, Weis sold the 78-acre property off Moyer Road to Howard in 1992.

Howard has built on the Weis family success by adding dining facilities, a restored carriage house banquet hall and a bed and breakfast cottage to the site, which remains an independent entity, wholly separate from NLC holdings.

The NLC partnership is now making its own mark in the Niagara wine industry, building on an industry tradition of excellence with bold plans to provide a new source of crisp, satisfying wines.

▶

*The award-winning partners, clockwise from bottom left: Hermann Weis, Paul Mazza, Dieter Jahnke and John Howard.*
– PHOTO BY DAVID GRUGGEN

*Success Stories*

# Niagara Land Company

Success 17 Stories

– PHOTO BY DENNIS MCGREAL

## CHAPTER 2

# The Hub Of The Horseshoe

# The Hub Of The Horseshoe

Where are our success stories coming from? Let's take a more in-depth look at the greater economic region which takes in a slightly larger area than the famed Golden Horseshoe urban sprawl winding around the tip of Lake Ontario, from Niagara Falls to Oakville.

By the late 1990s, the population of the Regional Municipality of Hamilton-Wentworth alone exceeded 470,000 people – more than 320,000 of them being residents of the City of Hamilton itself. Add in the interdependent and inter-connected populations of Halton and Niagara regions, and the total population of this vast economic region exceeds 1 million.

This region's borders are somewhat elastic and can include the lands between lakes Ontario and Erie, including Haldimand-Norfolk region to Hamilton's south and Brant County to the west.

This vast land mass, dubbed the Great Big Area, adds over 250,000 people to this community of communities, this Hamilton-centred hinterland of shared geography and economic interests. It incorporates everything from heavy industry to financial and commercial interests, to one of the nation's few areas capable of growing soft fruits.

Co-ordinating and orchestrating prosperity in such a diverse region hasn't been easy. Municipalities, regions and chambers of commerce in this area have represented their own interests over the years while occasionally addressing the challenge of formulating a joint strategy for the larger community of shared interest.

In recent years, this challenge has been taken up by I-COR, the Interlake Corridor, a not-for-profit organization representing the economic development interests of the various municipalities between lakes Erie and Ontario, within its sphere of influence.

I-COR is intent on overcoming isolationism among individual communities, encouraging businesses to grow beyond immediate municipal markets and borders, and getting the municipalities to work together to efficiently rebuild and expand the area economy.

The challenge has also been taken up by Renaissance, also a not-for-profit corporation, founded in 1994 as a partnership of business, government and academic leaders.

Renaissance seeks to help develop new enterprises, foster research and innovation, establish new ways of networking, promote co-operation between economic sectors and assist firms in exporting abroad. The emphasis is on moving forward.

"Renaissance was born from a feeling our future as a vibrant, self-sufficient metropolitan area was slipping away," says former Renaissance vice chairman Jake Doherty, noting "nationally there is a tendency to dismiss Hamilton as a gritty suburb of Toronto whose needs can be serviced from Bay and Yonge."

"The recession of the '90s was preceded by a tidal wave of downsizing and restructuring of our major manufacturing industries – many believed that Canada's industrial heartland was in danger of becoming a rustbelt," adds Doherty, who spent several years developing Renaissance into an effective, thought-provoking entity before leaving to pursue other goals in the summer of 1997.

"At the same time, the Greater Toronto Area – the GTA – was suffocating or swallowing up many of our service and retail businesses. My understanding is that there has been a substantial net drain of consumer spending from our market for some time."

Doherty notes the Hamilton Census Metropolitan Area (yet another Hamilton-centred economic region) has, in recent years, enjoyed the lowest or second lowest unemployment rates in the country. By the fall of 1997, the unemployment rate had fallen to 6.4 per cent in the Hamilton CMA taking in Hamilton-Wentworth region, Burlington and Grimsby. The drop was due, in no small part, to a strengthening local economy which generated an astonishing 16,000 new jobs since the spring.

"Most of us, however, sense the unemployment figures would be much higher if we included the number of people who dropped out of the workforce, or whose skills are under-utilized," Doherty cautions. He points out that Renaissance has attempted to grapple with issues of public good versus private self interest and long-term planning versus short-term expediency.

"Do we simply let the market sort out these issues with Adam Smith's invisible hand," he asks, "or do we take charge of the bridge-building challenge and create the collaborative networks required to give us a more certain sense of direction?"

Clearly, Renaissance has chosen the latter course. Noting that the Renaissance mandate is to "address the structural barriers inhibiting job and wealth creation," Doherty observes that: "With a small staff and many volunteers we've positioned ourselves to be a coalition of coalitions and broker between government, business and academia."

"In many respects, our role is structural – identifying barriers to growth, putting new solutions in place with the help of our growth committees and telling the world all the good things that are happening here. There's a perception problem – but we're working to overcome that."

In correcting barriers to growth, Renaissance has its work cut out for it. For one of the major growth barriers – easily identified but difficult to resolve – is the lack of access to risk capital by small entrepreneurs, the leading source of job creation.

"Lots of capital around," Doherty observes, "but there is a general agreement that it isn't flowing to owners of small firms, particularly those looking for less than about $750,000."

"This is an important issue because conventional wisdom says most job growth comes from small and medium-size companies – and we need more of them to offset the downsizing of our large companies. We also need to champion the imagination and vigour of the individual entrepreneur."

Some of the companies Doherty refers to are featured in this book and are listed in a helpful business directory contained at the back of the book.

▶

*A restored Gore Park fountain is the centrepiece of Hamilton's core. The fountain, a Sesquicentennial project, exemplifies the spirit of confidence and optimism taking hold in the downtown.*
*– PHOTO BY DAVID GRUGGEN*

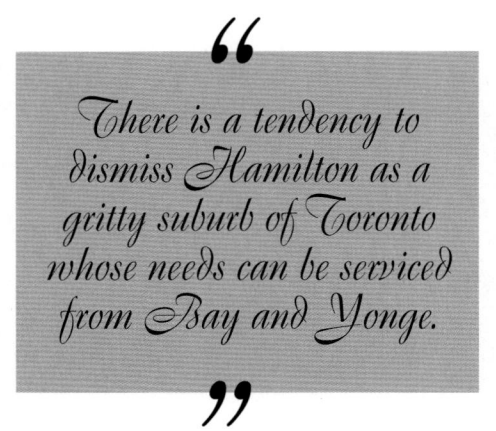

> "There is a tendency to dismiss Hamilton as a gritty suburb of Toronto whose needs can be serviced from Bay and Yonge."

*Success Stories*

# The Hub Of The Horseshoe

*Success* 21 *Stories*

# The Hub Of The Horseshoe

To help address the need for capital for small to mid-sized businesses, a spin-off of Renaissance known as Renaissance Community Investments has received a $600,000 grant from Industry Canada under its Canada Community Investment Plan.

These operating funds, along with funds raised locally, would allow Renaissance to help firms get their business plans ready while providing management advice through the BAC (Business Advisory Centre). Renaissance screens requests for financing and puts companies in touch with qualified investors and lenders.

"Capital alone is often not enough," Doherty notes, adding that "usually a small firm needs an infusion of management experience."

Doherty anticipates there will be a wide variety of needs to be met from the GBA's population of more than 1 million people representing "a range of economic assets that probably cannot be matched in Canada – steelmaking to greenhouses, great wines and high-tech visionaries."

Nick Catalano, economic development director for Hamilton-Wentworth region, is determined to help the region realize its impressive potential.

Catalano is focusing on how Hamilton-Wentworth can best take advantage of its enviable physical position at the hub of one of North America's most densely populated international markets.

Within a 500-mile radius of the region, only about a day's drive, is a total market population of 120 million people.

And, Greater Hamilton's costs of doing business are much lower than those of Toronto and many of the American centres within this 500-mile sphere, giving Hamilton a competitive cost advantage which has yet to be fully exploited.

One impediment to growth is the city's lingering image as a purely industrial centre. That image, never really accurate from the beginning, is today glaringly at odds with the Hamilton reality of a diversified economy led by health care and environmental services. "Awareness is our number one problem in promoting this region," Catalano admits. "We still have a long way to go to get the message out that ours is a diversified economy."

"Steel, God willing, will always be the cornerstone of our economy," asserts Catalano, who speaks with awe of Dofasco's $600 million investment in hot mill technology and $60 million spent on computers, all part of its ongoing multi-billion-dollar infrastructure investment program.

"But although Stelco and Dofasco are individually the largest employers, steel is no longer the leading employment sector – in fact, the steel sector ranks fifth overall," he adds.

Catalano explains that the health care sector has become the new leading source of employment, followed by environmental services, secondary manufacturing, transportation services and warehousing – and then the steel and primary metals sector.

The hospitality sector is also huge, according to Catalano, accounting for some 10,000 local jobs, but this sector is often classified under separate headings such as hotels, restaurants and food and beverage sectors.

Manufacturing alone accounts for nearly 100,000 jobs and is the "backbone of the economy," says Catalano.

Catalano notes while the steelmakers have downsized, cutting their workforces in half in the past decade, the economic region's diversification has meant that many displaced workers are finding new homes in other expanding sectors such as environmental services. For example, in just the past few years, Philip Services Inc. has grown from fewer than 200 employees to over 1,000 local employees within an international workforce of 12,000 people.

"And Philip's headquarters are right across the street from my office – they're a made-in-Hamilton success story," he enthuses.

"Our strengths include our diversification, our highly trained labour pool, our access to skilled labour and high-tech expertise."

The Hamilton CMA is itself a prosperous marketplace, boasting $4.5 billion worth of retail sales each year while industry giants such as Stelco, Dofasco, Laidlaw and Philip Services measure their sales in the billions of dollars. Blessed with one of Canada's lowest rates of unemployment, the Hamilton CMA's average per capita income at about $20,000 per individual, ranks 6 per cent above the national average.

> "Within a 500-mile radius of the region, only about a day's drive, is a total market population of 120 million people."

Vision 2020, prepared by the regional Chairman's Task Force on Sustainable Development with input from 1,000 local citizens, sees a community of industry, transportation services and green spaces working in inter-connected harmony.

Achieving that vision is an ongoing goal of Catalano and many others who recognize Hamilton's strengths and weaknesses and understand that by overcoming the city's problems, the region as a whole can advance into new levels of prosperity.

Beyond Hamilton's lingering, limited and badly outdated image as a purely industrial town, is the city's physical limitation. Simply put, it's grown all it possibly can within its existing boundaries so any growth must come from within through the redevelopment of developed lands.

"Hamilton really doesn't have any greenfield sites, that is, sites which have never been developed before for any purpose," says Catalano. "That's meant we've had to develop from within brownfield sites that once were used for something else, such as industrial uses, and may be contaminated and limited in their use."

And there's a struggling downtown core.

"One of the things that has to be recognized about the downtown core right now is that it's a destination location," says Catalano, "and unless you live there, you're not likely to go there unless there's a (AHL) Bull Dogs game or some other attraction to draw you there. Hamilton has more per capita mall space than virtually any other comparable community in Canada – and that has to be hurting the downtown stores as well."

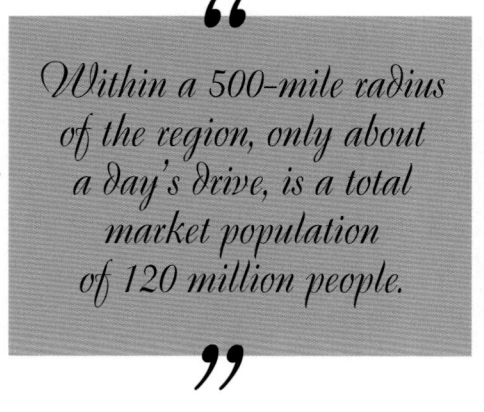

# The Hub Of The Horseshoe

*Downtown Hamilton has some problems, say experts, but the problems are solvable and the potential for the city's core is great.*
— PHOTO BY DENNIS MCGREAL

All of this has served to depress property prices in the core – a reality some would see as a negative trait. But that's only one way of looking at this situation. "There are phenomenal opportunities downtown," Catalano asserts. "The realty prices are low, the problems are solvable and the potential is great."

To help realize the city and region's potential, Catalano and his department regularly put their heads together with Renaissance, the Hamilton & District Chamber of Commerce, Hamilton City Hall, GHTEC (Greater Hamilton Technology Enterprise Centre) McMaster University, Mohawk College and dozens of top business people giving freely of their time and expertise.

"It's a terrific alliance," Catalano says proudly. "There are no turf wars, just a common desire to solve our common problems and help our community prosper."

"There's a strong sense of everyone working together to face common challenges – you don't find that in very many communities," asserts Lee Kirkby, the former executive director of the Hamilton and District Chamber of Commerce.

The chamber also gave birth to another Hamilton institution – the Hamilton Better Business Bureau – which operated under the aegis of the local chamber from 1938 through to the mid-1970s.

Today, the local BBB annually fields an average of 45,000 inquiries, 6,000 telephoned complaints and some 1,450 written complaints. Serving the Hamilton-Wentworth, Burlington and Niagara regions, the local BBB regularly promotes business ethics and is a dependable source of business-oriented information.

As the hub of a far greater economic region, Hamilton's heart needs to beat more vigorously. The failing or improving health of Greater Hamilton has a profound impact on the body of the larger region. Doherty, Catalano and others give reason for confidence Hamilton's economy will continue to grow more vibrant.

Another reason for confidence lies with the growing number of success stories to be discovered in the greater economic region.

Success can be measured in terms of a vast increase in profit, a winning business strategy, the capturing of a lucrative market niche – or simply remaining solvent and turning the corner in tough economic times.

We'll encounter an array of success stories in this book, all of them different, all compelling, and all offering a window on the approaches taken to achieve what all of us want: success.

*Success Stories*

*The Hub Of The Horseshoe*

*Success* 24 *Stories*

# The Hub Of The Horseshoe

*The Royal Connaught Howard Johnson Hotel has been a Hamilton landmark for more than 80 years. With its stately charm, the 'Grand Old Lady of Hamilton' is a key part of the city's downtown and remains one of Canada's finest hotels.*
– PHOTO BY DAVID GRUGGEN

*The Sheraton Hamilton Hotel is another jewel in the heart of Hamilton. The five-star, four diamond facility is connected to Jackson Square and the Hamilton Convention Centre.*
– PHOTO BY DENNIS MCGREAL

*Success Stories*

# Hamilton & District Chamber Of Commerce

Creating opportunity since 1845. That's the slogan and the simple statement of fact that continues to drive the Hamilton and District Chamber of Commerce. For more than 150 years, the chamber has generated networking opportunities, insightful, educational forums, economic data, promotional events and numerous opportunities for companies to expand their business.

"The chamber has always focused on being the catalyst to help people achieve success," asserts 1997-1998 Chamber President Bob Swenor. "We also maintain good ties with McMaster University, Mohawk College and the public sector because we know that we can often work together to address the challenges facing our community," he adds.

"Our essential role has been, from the beginning, to help businesses and individuals in the community be successful."

Swenor notes the chamber has become more outward looking over the years and is currently involved as a partner in the Canada-United States BorderNet Alliance, a regional network of business organizations devoted to the development of tourism, trade and investment in the bi-national area linking Hamilton, Toronto, Buffalo and Rochester, New York.

The chamber's success at promoting the local business community and providing it with relevant information and opportunities is reflected in its rising membership. In 1995, the chamber looked back fondly on 150 years of tireless efforts to promote business and civic concerns, foster growth and develop generations of entrepreneurs.

Over 1,000 companies – and over 1,700 individual members – now belong to the Hamilton chamber, a milestone which Swenor deems: "an outstanding achievement that took a lot of effort by many people."

And the chamber's ongoing success is pegged to its central role in fostering the growth of Hamilton's traditional role as a major commercial centre.

From very early in its history, Hamilton was a thriving centre of trade and commerce – a heritage that continues through to today. In fact, in 1845 – a year before the City of Hamilton was incorporated – the bustling community had already established the Hamilton Board of Trade, the forerunner of today's Hamilton and District Chamber of Commerce.

The board of trade had been an early supporter of free trade with the United States, although it reversed that position in 1910 in an effort to protect Hamilton manufacturers. Almost 80 years later the chamber would again support freer trade with the Americans.

In 1903, the board pushed for civic improvements such as additional drinking fountains. It also formed an alliance with Hamilton's Trades and Labor Council to arbitrate an end to a costly Teamsters strike hurting the local economy.

> "The chamber has always been front and centre when it comes to addressing the legitimate concerns of business and community."

And, in 1920 another milestone was reached when the board reconstituted itself as the Hamilton Chamber of Commerce and quickly took on such successful projects as relocating McMaster University from Toronto to Hamilton and bringing about the Chedoke Golf Course.

During the Great Depression of the Dirty 1930s, the chamber demonstrated considerable compassion for the less fortunate members of Hamilton society. The chamber initiated a system of garden plots allowing the unemployed to grow produce. And it raised funds to cover rent owed by needy citizens.

From 1939-1945, the chamber supported the Second World War effort by organizing massive donations of foodstuffs and gifts for the City of Hamilton Tiger Squadron, a bomber squadron manned by local volunteers fighting overseas.

As Hamilton celebrated its centennial in 1946, the chamber played its usual active role, promoting, among other major events, the first Miss Canada Pageant.

In the 1980s, the chamber could be found supporting the Corporate Challenge event, Crimestoppers and a Chinese chamber to attract Asian investment.

In the 1990s, it remained active, speaking out on tax issues, government budgets and legislative concerns while bringing a lengthy list of prominent business leaders and speakers to the city to address everything from business strategies to exports and international trade.

During Hamilton's Sesquicentennial in 1996, the chamber contributed enormously to making this a successful year. Among the chamber's many achievements was the introduction of a commemorative Sesquicentennial coin created by Ancaster sculptor Elizabeth Holbrook.

The chamber's tireless promotion of business community concerns may be having a subtle impact. In 1997, the Globe & Mail's Report on Business magazine ranked the Hamilton area as the 6th best community in which one can do business in Canada. The area is also finally gaining recognition as a major export centre in which the bulk of more than 700 manufacturers are involved in exporting. In fact, over 50 per cent of everything produced in Greater Hamilton is exported.

Clearly the chamber's message – that this is a great place to do business – is finally getting out to the national media. The need to repeat this to wider audiences has been taken to heart by the chamber's many members who play a leadership role in building our economic region.

In this role, they appear to be inspired by their first president Isaac Buchanan, who noted back in 1845 that "without the committed leadership of those who strive to build an economy, our community will cease to strengthen and grow."

And this historic role is now being championed by a new generation of chamber members.

"The chamber has always been front and centre when it comes to addressing the legitimate concerns of business and the community," notes Swenor.

"Our history and our future are closely tied to making our business community – and the wider community beyond that – as successful as possible."

▶

*Hamilton's Chamber of Commerce has been a guiding light, creating business opportunities in the city since 1845.*
*– PHOTO BY DENNIS MCGREAL*

Success Stories

# Hamilton & District Chamber Of Commerce

*Success* 27 *Stories*

– PHOTO BY DAVID GRUGGEN

# CHAPTER 3

# Industry & Transportation

# Industry & Transportation

"It's very hard to quantify the magnitude of the economic contribution industry has made to this region," says Neil Everson, manager of business development for Hamilton-Wentworth Economic Development Department.

"I believe it's generally acknowledged that the one-mile strip along Burlington Street East – taking in Stelco, Dofasco, Procter & Gamble and others – is the most productive mile in Canada," adds Everson. "As a source of wealth generation, this mile-long strip may be the biggest single contributor to Canada's Gross National Product."

Lee Kirkby explains that the enduring, resilient strength of Hamilton's industrial base sets it apart from other industrial areas, particularly the failed rustbelt regions of the United States.

"Heavy industry is still a major part of our economy – and I expect it always will be," asserts Kirkby, the former executive director of the Hamilton and District Chamber of Commerce.

"Our industrial base wasn't destroyed as industry was elsewhere," adds Kirkby, whose familiarity with industry is based in part on eight years as the chamber's executive director. "In fact, in some ways, it was strengthened by the competitive forces that obliterated industry in other places," notes Kirkby, who left the chamber in 1997 to become manager of the image documenting department at Leppert Business Equipment.

"Our heavy industry has downsized in some cases to become more competitive," Kirkby notes. "But unlike many other North American centres, we've been able to retain a substantial part of our economy based on heavy to light industry," he adds.

"Some North American cities have been left with no industrial base. But somehow we've been able to nurture our traditional industries and create some new industries as a result – Philip Services comes to mind – and that has been a real success story for this community."

Kirkby also points to the enduring role of Hamilton's steelmakers, as evidence of the economic region's ability to house vibrant new companies while retaining industrial giants.

Much of the attention given to the economic contribution of Stelco and Dofasco tends to focus on the fact that both Hamilton-based giant steelmakers are multi-billion-dollar corporations, rank among Canada's biggest companies and remain the two largest individual employers in the Hamilton area.

Stelco and Dofasco each employ approximately 7,000 people, contribute enormously to local causes and invest literally billions of dollars in their Hamilton facilities.

For the second quarter of 1997, ended June 30, Stelco reported a $43 million profit, up 26.4 per cent from $34 million for the same three-month period in 1996.

Stelco second-quarter 1997 sales revenue rang in at a record $819 million, up 3.3 per cent from $793 million in 1996.

Dofasco's second-quarter profit was $65.8 million, up 20.5 per cent from $54.6 million. Revenue for the quarter was $793.3 million, up from $787.7 million. And that's just a single quarter. Both big steelmakers measure annual revenue in the billions of dollars – and they ship millions of tons of steel annually.

To these heady statistics, Everson adds another: The fact that 18 per cent of shipping on the Great Lakes system is directly due to Stelco and Dofasco.

By the fall of 1997, Statistics Canada reported the primary metals industry was running at more than 90 per cent capacity. Dofasco spokesman Peter Earle described the steelmaker as running flat out to keep up with demand in a strengthening economy.

"Measuring the full economic contribution of the steelmakers is also difficult," Everson acknowledges, "because in addition to their very visible direct contribution, there are many spin-off benefits from these companies which purchase and sell a lot of goods and services locally. Both big steelmakers," he explains, "are very loyal to the local community."

Everson also points to the literally hundreds of smaller industries which together create thousands of jobs. Many of these companies are heavily involved in exporting and they too play a beneficial, productive role in community life.

A striking example of a successful, small industry can be found at Dominion Pattern Works where company President Dan Peace heads a dedicated group of pattern makers. In addition to his contribution to the local economy and employment rolls, Dan Peace and his father Gordon Peace share many decades of dedicated involvement as Scouts Canada youth leaders.

As Scoutmaster of 4th Ancaster Scouts, I know of the Peace family's tireless efforts in the field of youth development. Dan Peace can usually be found on the reviewing stand with other Scouts supporters, including my mother, Pearl Davie, in her role as past president of the Hamilton Community Credit Union, major sponsors of the annual Scouts/Guides Parade in Hamilton, the largest such youth parade in North America.

Dan Peace and Dominion Pattern Works are finding success by focusing on the most promising niches in a shrinking market for industrial patterns. After losing some major customers which went out of business, Peace fought back with an aggressive effort to secure new customers in Canada and the U.S. We'll take a closer look at his compelling success story later in this chapter.

We'll also take a detailed look at Philip Services and the inspiring success story of company founders and brothers, Allen and Philip Fracassi. Beyond these upcoming profiles, anyone wishing to research further information on the companies and organizations referred to throughout this book, are welcome to utilize the directory at the back of this publication.

> *Heavy industry is still a major part of our economy ... Our industrial base wasn't destroyed as it was elsewhere.*

▶ *The Welland Canal is a major shipping corridor, joining lakes Erie and Ontario to the entire Great Lakes shipping system.*
– PHOTO BY DENNIS MCGREAL

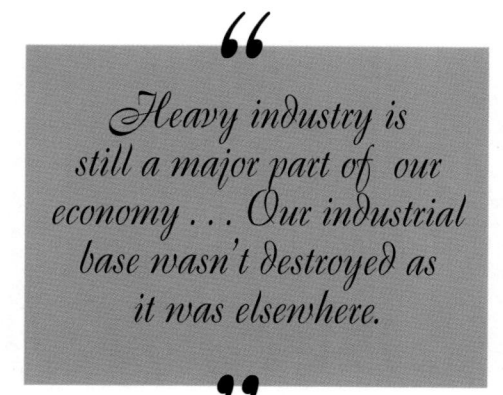

# Industry & Transportation

Success Stories

## Industry & Transportation

**K**ey to success of industry and commerce is the ability to cost-effectively move goods and services to markets and customers. Here, our Hamilton-centred economic region enjoys enviable access to the Great Lakes shipping corridors, including the St. Lawrence Seaway and Welland Canal systems.

We have access to the Queen Elizabeth Way and Highways 403 and 401, numerous secondary highways and upcoming freeways. Our airport is fast becoming a leading cargo port and we're seeing increasing success in the air passengers business.

Everson believes the Hamilton area transportation network is one of the economic region's biggest selling points.

"We have a cost-competitive, accessible and efficient system of road, rail, air and port facilities to move people and goods quite effectively," Everson notes.

Kirkby agrees with this assessment, noting that "to some extent our transportation network is really coming into its own."

"We have good transferability of transport modes, shipping is showing greater potential to grow now than it has in recent years – and we're marketing our transportation system better," Kirkby adds. "Hamilton has long been the hub of a telecommunications, shipping, air and ground transportation system and we're on the cusp of seeing paybacks with a strengthening economy."

"If we want to fully capture the benefits, we have to look at how to strategically align and market these components of our network," Kirkby explains, "including marketing the fact that our facilities such as the airport and our roadways have far less congestion than Toronto, meaning you can move goods and services more efficiently."

"How we find the most effective ways to cross-market our harbour and our airport, for example, presents us with as many challenges as opportunities," Kirkby notes. "But the potential benefits are enormous."

Indeed, the network Kirkby refers to can also been seen as an economic circulation system, flowing the life blood of commerce along highway arteries, river veins and air corridors.

Road transportation has been assisted significantly with the fall 1997 opening of the east-west portion of the Redhill Freeway, known as The Linc. The north-south portion is to open in 2001.

One missing link, however, is the completion of a perimeter road to join the Queen Elizabeth Way Niagara to Highway 403. This roadway, which would likely incorporate Industrial Drive, would provide the final piece of a ring roadway surrounding the city of Hamilton. The perimeter road is not expected to be undertaken until the year 2008 or later.

"Most major cities have a ring road – and we don't," Everson laments. "But we're working on it, we're getting there. Eventually, you will be able to circle the entire city and access the city from the nearest corridor to where you want to travel."

While ground transportation is coming into its own, Hamilton International Airport has already achieved an impressive level of success – which seems to be building up on a daily basis.

Everson ranks among Hamilton International Airport's biggest admirers. He points to rising passenger traffic levels and a seven-fold increase in air cargo traffic in the span of a year.

He expects the $17.2 million UPS investment at the airport will lead to further growth as more courier business is directed to an airport with little congestion and no flight curfews. "Air transport is really taking off – it's just flying," says Everson.

A brief laugh is followed by an apologetic "pardon the puns."

Everson is equally enthusiastic about Hamilton Harbour, noting that the Port of Hamilton is a far busier shipping facility than its Toronto counterpart.

The self-supporting Hamilton Harbour Commissioners are also taking a multifaceted approach when it comes to earning revenue.

In addition to the usual port fees to harbour users, the HHC is leasing some of its waterfront industrial lands to commercial

## Industry & Transportation

tenants, creating an informal – and highly successful – industrial park, injecting new vitality into an industrial zone.

The harbour is also home to McKeil Marine, a long-established, family owned business which is achieving great success with its imaginative business approach.

Using tugs and barges to perform work more usually associated with lakers, McKeil is capturing a significant share of cargo transportation markets.

We'll also take a closer look at McKeil, the HHC and the Hamilton airport in profiles later in this chapter. The success of these transportation leaders make one thing perfectly clear: By land, sea and air, our economic region is open for business.

▲
*While there's much more to Hamilton than steel, it's difficult to ignore the key role that Stelco and Dofasco continue to play in stimulating the local economy. Together, Stelco and Dofasco are directly responsible for providing some 14,000 local jobs. Stelco's Hilton Works is shown in a night-time shot above.*

Success Stories

# Philip Services

Driven by the shared vision of the entrepreneurial Fracassi brothers, Philip Services Corp. is today the North American industrial services leader.

Hamilton-based Philip – after a 1997 merger with Allwaste and Serv-Tech firms – achieved estimated 1997 revenue of $2.1 billion, tripling the $700 million in revenue the firm achieved just two years earlier. From less than $60 million in 1988, revenue has been growing by a staggering 2,700 per cent annually.

All told, Philip has over 300 North American locations employing a total of 12,000 people, over 1,000 of them in the Hamilton area. And, with 102 million shares outstanding, Philip's total market capitalization is over $2.5 billion.

It's an awe-inspiring success story for a company which didn't go public until 1991 and traces its roots to the north end Hamilton backyard of brothers Allen and Philip Fracassi.

The Fracassi brothers had shared a childhood of hard work in a family which immigrated to Canada from Italy in 1965. They laboured after school and weekends in their backyard, maintaining trucks owned by their father, Enzo Fracassi, who ran a haulage firm from their home.

After his father's business went bankrupt in the late 1970s, Allen Fracassi borrowed $20,000 and bought the trucks.

He soon realized that scrap steel contained in waste sands could be screened out and resold – and he set up a backyard screening operation.

The early emphasis on waste reuse and recycling was borne of necessity: Although the firm began as Philip Enterprises in 1980, as an industrial waste handling-disposal firm, it didn't acquire its first landfill site until 1988.

To avoid paying the owners of other landfill sites steep fees to dump their customers' wastes, the company tried to divert as much material as possible away from landfill. It sold the foundry sand it was hauling to cement factories as a substitute raw material.

"We did it partly to cut costs," recalls Allen Fracassi, Philip's President and Chief Executive Officer, noting that his company was able to profit in two ways – from waste haulage fees and from revenue raised by selling waste as raw material.

"By recycling and reselling a lot of the waste materials, we earned additional revenue and cut the landfill expense."

From these entrepreneurial roots and talent for converting waste into raw material, the company – named after the brothers' grandfather – would grow into a diversified recycling giant.

Indeed, where others see refuse, the Fracassis see revenue. Together, they've made Philip North America's leading provider of resource recovery and industrial services – and one of Canada's fastest-growing firms.

> "We recognize the need to focus heavily on technology, to make sure we never fall behind and that we're the ones leading the way."

"There's really no such thing as waste, just materials we can recycle and resell," notes Allen Fracassi. "We always ask: 'What can I do with it?' – rather than 'How can I get rid of it?'"

That philosophy is shared by his brother Philip, Executive Vice-President and Chief Operating Officer, who observes "one company's waste is another company's raw material."

Two years after achieving its 1991 stock market listing, the company formed its Metals Recovery Group on acquiring Hamilton firms: Waxman Resources, the innovative plastics and cable recycler; and I.W.& S. Ferrous, Canada's second largest ferrous scrap recycler.

Metals Recovery Group President Robert Waxman notes revenue from the Group has gone from $308 million in 1995 to $1.3 billion in 1997.

That same year, the company acquired the Luntz Corp., Intsel Southwest Partnership, Conversion Resources Inc. and Warrenton Resources Inc. in the U.S.; and the Alcan Alloys plant at Guelph.

The 1990s also marked the acquisition of Nortru, a recycler of waste oils, sludges and solvents with operations in Detroit and Texas; and Burlington Environmental with five chemical recycling plants in the Pacific Northwest.

In 1994, the company founded Philip Utilities which soon secured a $187 million contract to operate several sewage and water treatment plants of Hamilton-Wentworth region. This private-public partnership is the first of its kind in Canada and largest in North America.

The company also named Hamilton as the site of a plant to recover zinc, lead and iron products in electric arc furnace residue created in steel production.

"This process clearly represents our approach to treating industrial by-products as raw material," notes Allen Fracassi. "We are able to produce materials with valuable reuse applications and provide viable alternatives to disposal."

In the fall of 1997, Philip opened a $4.5 million polyurethane recycling plant in Detroit in alliance with BASF, one of the world's largest chemical companies, to turn bumpers, steering wheels and other plastic auto parts into reusable material. This plant will divert thousands of tons of automotive plastics from landfill sites.

Also in the fall of 1997, Philip acquired Hamilton-based Intermetco, the largest ferrous metal recycler in Canada with 1996 revenue of almost $200 million.

This acquisition will help Philip penetrate the southeastern U.S. market and expand the company's steel processing and distribution capabilities.

Over the years, the original solid waste business ceased to dominate a company which had diversified into an industrial services firm providing services in by-product processing, metals recovery and technical services. Philip sold its solid waste business in 1996.

After operating for six years as Philip Environmental, the company changed its name to Philip Services Corp. in 1997 to better reflect its evolving role as North America's premier provider of integrated industrial services.

"We introduced the concept of creating a 'new box' – a new market sector called resource recovery and industrial services," notes Lynda Kuhn, vice-president corporate communications. "It was a radically new concept, but as we talked to the financial community and our customers, it became clear they had us pigeon-holed

# Philip Services

*Philip is a leading provider of resource recovery and industrial services. Here, Philip provides industrial vacuum service at CN's Locomotive Reliability Centre in Toronto.*

as a waste management company," Kuhn recalls. "It also became clear that our old name was reinforcing that perception."

"The Allwaste and Serv-Tech mergers were the perfect opportunity to establish a new, more appropriate identity," she adds.

"These Houston-based companies added approximately $500 million (US) in revenue and established Philip in the industrial services sector."

Philip is now organized as two operating divisions: Industrial Services Group, taking in Philip's By-Products Recovery and Environmental Services operations, plus Serv-Tech and Allwaste; and the Metals Recovery Group, encompassing Philip's steel, copper, aluminum and plastics processing operations.

About 80 per cent of Philip's employees and revenues are in the U.S. In late 1997, Philip established Pittsburgh as its U.S. corporate headquarters. "When I got off the plane in Pittsburgh, I was immediately reminded of home," says Allen Fracassi, who reaffirms Philip's world headquarters will remain in Hamilton.

Philip provides extensive consulting services, analyzing the customer's production process to find ways to minimize waste generation. For remaining waste that can't be eliminated, Philip uses its technology to help the customer reuse or recycle as much of this waste as possible.

While Allen Fracassi continues to demonstrate an impressive knack for acquiring good-fit companies, Philip Fracassi brings operations experience and leadership to the fore – developing the company from within while managing a diverse group of operations.

"We work in tandem," Philip Fracassi says of the successful, brotherly, entrepreneurial management arrangement.

"While Allen works on acquisitions, my focus is on developing what we've got and enlarging it – I like to keep very focused on our margins," he notes.

"And," Fracassi points out, "we both recognize the need to focus heavily on technology, to make sure we never fall behind and that we're the ones leading the way with the right technology."

*Success Stories*

# Dominion Pattern Works

In Canada, throughout the United States, perhaps one day in all of Europe, you'll find Peace.

Dominion Pattern Works president Dan Peace and his staff of highly skilled and motivated pattern-makers are placing a greater emphasis on exporting the foundry tooling they make in Hamilton.

They initially turned to exports to weather a tightening domestic market. But Peace and his staff are finding shipments abroad hold the potential for helping them do much better than merely surviving in lean economic times.

In fact, Dominion Pattern Works is counting on exports to play an even bigger role in the company's future prosperity. Success and growth are being achieved by expanding horizons and "looking a little further afield for sales," explains Peace.

"We'd like to expand our market presence further into the U.S. and Europe in the future," adds, the amiable president of Dominion Pattern Works.

"The market has increased in size with the improving economy – the U.S. and European markets are huge," notes Peace, who currently sells tooling primarily to firms located in Southern Ontario, with the American Midwest making up his second-biggest market.

"The lower Canadian dollar helps us fish in the big U.S. pond, along with many others in the Canadian exporting economy," notes Peace in an interview at his 5,000-square-foot plant on Princess Street in central Hamilton.

Dominion Pattern Works doubled its manufacturing space in 1997 with the acquisition of two neighbouring buildings.

The company now boasts a total of 10,000 square feet of space dedicated to the manufacturing of patterns for locomotive parts, rolling stock, valves, mining equipment, power generation equipment and various components for pulp and paper and manufacturing industries.

The company is moving towards Computer Assisted Manufacturing and Rapid Proto-typing, a computer-driven system for building pattern equipment with increased accuracy and speed.

Peace notes that U.S. sales have been growing steadily. To build these sales, Dominion Pattern Works has devoted considerable resources to staff training and new equipment.

Revenue growth is being fueled by higher production tooling and computer assisted design work along with a versatile, skilled staff of 12 people with a combined total of over 400 years experience.

The company has increased sales each year. Major customers include Dominion Castings, Westinghouse Canada, General Motors and General Electric.

It's a remarkable turnaround for a firm which lost its biggest single customer – accounting for 25 per cent of sales – when Dofasco closed its steel castings foundry in the early 1990s. This blow followed

> *Pattern-making goes beyond science and skill. It's an artform and there's a lot of heart in the work we do.*

similar foundry closings over the years by International Harvester, Otis Elevator, Westinghouse Canada, Slater Steel, Canada Iron, and other companies throughout Hamilton and across Ontario.

As foundries closed, several pattern shops went under, leaving Dominion Pattern Works as the dominant player in a shrinking local market. But Peace fought back with aggressive marketing in the U.S., broadening his customer base and finding fresh sources of sales.

The American Midwest has proven a lucrative market for Dominion Pattern's wood, aluminum and urethane patterns and core boxes – used by foundries in moulding and casting an impressive array of railway and industrial equipment parts.

Dominion Pattern Works also has valuable non-ferrous customers making copper and aluminum castings for pulp and paper, mining and manufacturing industries.

In 1997, the company celebrated its 81st anniversary, attracting several new customers and participating more actively in the Canadian Foundry Association and the American Foundries Society.

His company's turnaround is a source of satisfaction for Dan Peace, who represents the third generation of pattern-makers to lead Dominion Pattern Works.

The small business was founded in 1916 by his grandfather, Harold V. Peace, and was later run by the founder's son, Gordon Peace, who retired in 1988, passing the torch to his son Dan.

Under the leadership of Dan Peace, Dominion Pattern Works developed a quality management system which met all the requirements for ISO 9001 registration and received this registration from the Quality Management Institute in 1996.

The Quality Management Institute has used the firm's self-designed quality system as an example for other North American firms to consider when pursuing their own ISO registration.

Dominion Pattern Works' quality management system, developed in-house by Peace and his staff, is only one example of the strides this progressive company has taken over the years. Witness, as well, the company's enduring, strong emphasis on efficient, high quality production, fast delivery times and strict adherence to meeting customer specifications.

The company has also invested heavily in computers and equipment upgrading to increase cost efficiencies and enhance overall quality. But Peace says the main reason for success can be found on the shop floor. "People are the key to our success," he notes. "We have always had a staff of gifted, hard-working pattern-makers who work as a team."

Dominion Pattern Works is also securing its future vitality by investing training time and resources in developing a new generation of pattern-makers, he notes. "We try to have at least one apprentice on our shop floor at all times."

Peace believes his talented staff have taken pattern-making to a higher level.

"This is very specialized work – our people can make just about anything.

"Pattern-making goes beyond science and skill. It's more than craftsmanship," he explains. "It's an artform and there's a lot of heart in the work we do."

▶
*Talent and technology have helped Dan Peace mold his company into a success in the challenging pattern-making field.*
– PHOTO BY DAVID GRUGGEN

# Dominion Pattern Works

Success Stories

# Hamilton International Airport

It truly is the hassle-free alternative. As I pull into one of the many free parking spaces at Hamilton International Airport, I'm just steps away from the terminal and departure counter.

Moments later, I'm boarding a plane, lifting off into clear blue skies and bidding a fond farewell to this convenient, modern airport located on the southern outskirts of Hamilton. And, I'm left wondering just how I ever coped in the past with the time-consuming congestion of Toronto's Pearson International Airport.

Hamilton International Airport is counting on air travellers, cargo carriers and courier companies to arrive at the same inescapable conclusion: It's simply the most convenient, inexpensive, easily accessible airport around.

Once the area's best-kept secret, the Hamilton International Airport is today a striking success story that began when the federal government retained ownership of 26 "national" airports while turning over about 70 "regional" airports to provinces or municipalities.

Owned by Hamilton-Wentworth, Hamilton International is the Crown Jewel of the Regionals, due to its modern infrastructure and its proximity to Toronto.

The airport's continuing turnaround accelerated in 1996 with the region's pivotal decision to turn operations over to private-sector management firm TradePort International Corporation, which is under contract through to the year 2036.

"The region decided, correctly, that the private sector could do a better job running the airport because it can make decisions and raise capital quickly," says TradePort president Tony Battaglia.

"And I saw a development opportunity to expand into the industrial-commercial sector," explains Battaglia, who is also president of Westpark Developments Inc. and a home builder since 1984.

Battaglia knew that he was flying into unfamiliar territory. His genius lay in marrying his own managerial skills with the specialized skill sets of a team of experts, including TradePort partners YVR Airport Services, a subsidiary of the Vancouver Airport Authority.

YVR provides consulting services and assists with airport management and operations while another TradePort partner, an independent Ready-Mix operator with experience at Pearson, is responsible for much of the airport's infrastructure construction work.

A third partner, LIUNA (Labourers International Union of North America) assists with financing construction work and overseeing employee relations, pension funds and other benefits. All of the partners are TradePort shareholders. Westpark is majority shareholder.

> *Once the area's best-kept secret, the Hamilton International Airport is today a striking success story.*

"The federal government has invested a lot of money in the airport over the years – especially in the 1980s, including its modern terminal building built in 1987," notes Battaglia. "But there has been little marketing of the airport over the years."

Battaglia has set about correcting this situation with a multimedia promotional campaign dubbing the Hamilton airport "your hassle-free alternative," and inviting people to "get a HUG" (Hamilton International User's Guide, available by calling toll-free: 1-888-757-1111).

The timing couldn't be better.

With over 25 million passengers a year, Pearson is badly congested and in need of the relief a second airport – Hamilton International – could provide.

Some relief is already kicking in with USAir. Other passenger carriers are expected to follow. Although Greyhound Air was discontinued after Laidlaw Inc. bought Greyhound's parent company, the former airline had achieved successful volumes and proved there is a market for its services. It's likely another passenger carrier will soon fill the void left by Greyhound. And for flights to the U.S., it's hard to beat the services of USAir and Hamilton International Airport.

Having personally used this airline and the airport, I have nothing but praise for its convenient, friendly and inexpensive service. USAir, an 11-year veteran at Hamilton International, has added a 30-passenger Saab 340 to its 19-passenger Jetstream. Thanks to USAir, the airport can now access 128 U.S. destinations.

In 1998, the airport will have expanded its main 8,000-foot runway to 10,000 feet – a prerequisite for attracting the large, overseas airlines.

TradePort has already made a financial commitment to undertake the project. Once the expansion is done, TradePort will begin a highly targeted campaign to convince key overseas airlines to reroute to Hamilton International.

Of the expanded runway, Battaglia borrows a phrase from Canadian author W. P. (Field of Dreams) Kinsella: "If you build it they will come."

"We're conducting scientific studies and devising a full-scale business plan which will show the airlines that they'll make more profit if they reroute to Hamilton," adds Battaglia.

The airport is also reaching out to a lucrative niche market through the multi-million-dollar Jetport facility now being built by Tim Hortons Donuts founder Ron Joyce, for the benefit of his own and other corporate jets. But the most lucrative area of business is cargo.

"This is a great location for the cargo carriers and courier companies," asserts Battaglia. "If you have to get a package to someone by the next morning, you usually can't get the job done out of Toronto because Pearson is not only congested, it has a night-time flying curfew."

"Here, there's no congestion or curfew. We operate 24-hours a day, with full customs service," he explains.

Major couriers – including United Parcel Service, Purolator Courier and Federal Express Canada – all operate out of Hamilton International Airport and have various expansion plans in the works, totalling many millions of dollars.

UPS alone announced a $17.2 million expansion, including a 47,800-square-foot operating facility. The move is one of the largest single investments ever made by a courier company in recent years. The facility is to open in the spring of 1998.

*Success Stories*

# Hamilton International Airport

*Cargo and passenger traffic are taking off at Hamilton International Airport, under TradePort president Tony Battaglia's leadership.*
– PHOTO BY DAVID GRUGGEN

Growth in the airport's cargo business has been truly phenomenal: From 9 million kilograms of cargo shipments in 1990, to over 60 million kilograms in 1995 and 72 million kilograms in 1996.

"Courier firms love our airport because they can fly at night and deliver the next morning," states Battaglia, who notes another source of increased cargo business is a trend favouring just-in-time delivery, allowing companies to bypass a costly build-up of inventory in a warehouse.

"The cargo business is also being expanded by people ordering goods over the Internet and by the importing and exporting needs of the local market," says Battaglia, adding TradePort designs, builds and leases back facilities to meet distribution and other needs of cargo carriers.

"Growth in cargo is a trend going well into the future. The airport is run entrepreneurially now and we have aggressive marketing campaigns needed to attract cargo carriers and airlines."

When TradePort took over the airport's management in 1996, 717 people already worked for the various companies making their home at the sprawling facility, located on the outskirts of Mount Hope.

A year later, over 800 people were employed by some 35 companies and the employment figure is expected to surpass 1,100 within 15 years, "and that's an ultra-conservative estimate," says Battaglia, "because if growth rates continue, we'll employ over 3,000 people by then."

There are already some 1,400 spin-off jobs, most of them high-paying positions.

TradePort conservatively estimates that there will be 2,500 direct and indirect jobs in 15 years. And, the total value of airport-related goods and services should surpass $527 million by then.

Battaglia sees the airport, harbour and highway system expanding Hamilton's role as the transportation and distribution hub of a vast metropolis stretching from Toronto to Niagara Falls.

"Hamilton has the perfect location," says Battaglia. "The airport will be our economic engine."

*Success Stories*

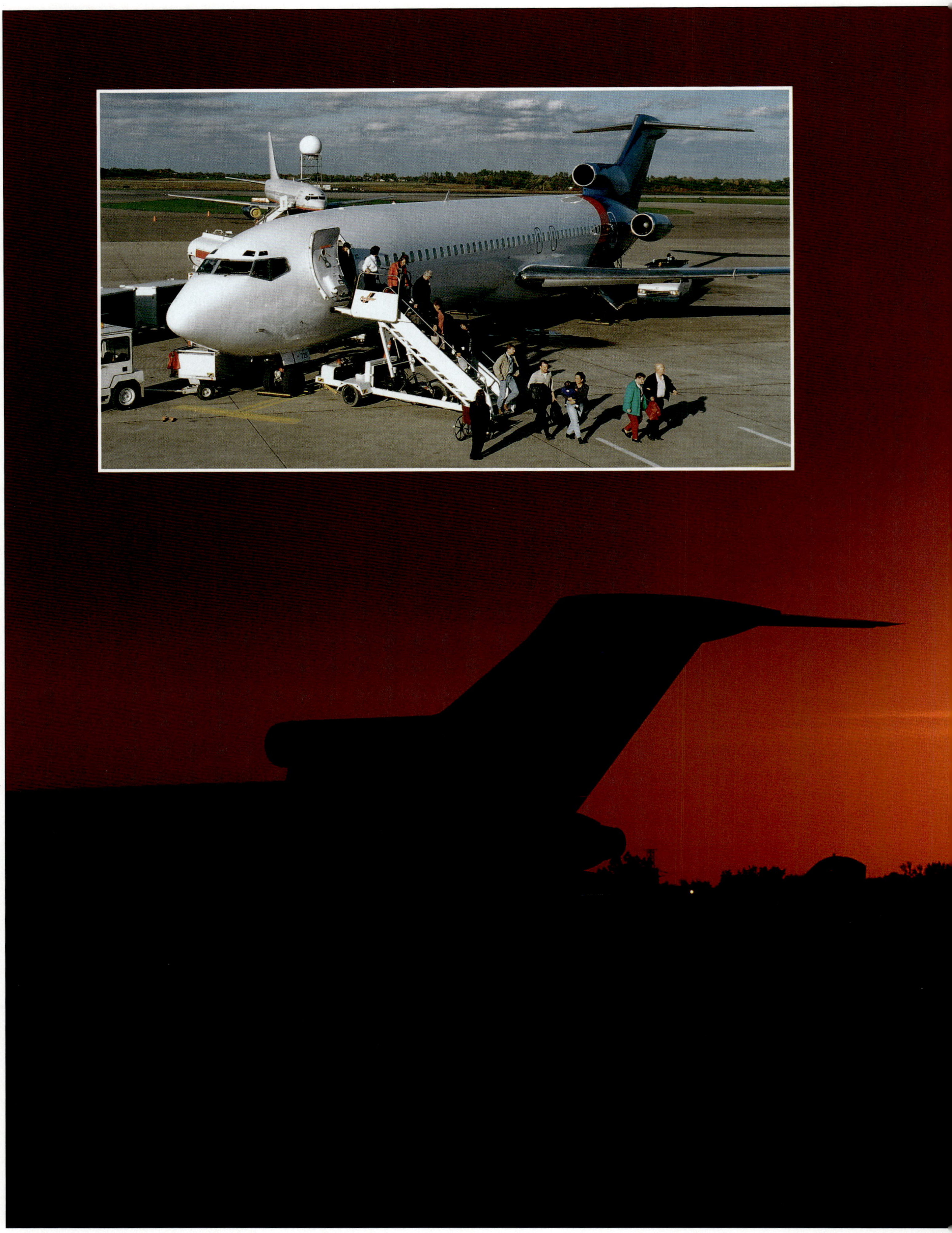

• *A new era dawned on the Hamilton International Airport when TradePort International took over management in 1996.*
– PHOTO BY DENNIS MCGREAL

# McKeil Marine

Blair McKeil strides across a basketball court, past a volleyball net, and towards a sound stage and soda fountains flanked by washrooms and a double-decker bus.

But the most impressive part of this scene is the location: The entire set-up is on the deck of a 400-ton barge floating on the calm waters of Hamilton Harbour.

"There's nothing like this anywhere," McKeil, 37, says with pride, "and while it's set up to entertain children right now, this barge can also be used as a platform to sell cars, military equipment, recreational vehicles, anything you want."

The youthful president of McKeil Marine Ltd., demonstrated the barge at Aquafest in July 1997, allowing local children to freely clamber over the deck, visit the soda fountain and climb through the authentic double-decker bus imported from England.

In addition to renting out the barge as a sales platform, McKeil intends to lease the 7,500-square-foot surface to firms holding business meetings on deck. It's also suitable for receptions, parties for 400 of your closest friends or as "a floating convention centre," notes McKeil.

And, for the convenience of guests dropping in, there's also a second-storey helicopter pad.

The range of imaginative uses for the 160-foot-long barge is typical of the innovative approach McKeil Marine is employing to venture into new markets and expand its business.

"We're diversifying our services, filling niche markets that tugs and barges were previously not used in," McKeil explains, "and growth has been in the transportation of commodities."

McKeil Marine is today active in transporting goods that traditionally have been carried by ships. Although a tug pushing a barge can be slower than a ship, the costs tend to be lower because the tug has a much smaller crew and lower operating costs. "We're moving slowly into transportation, building up our market presence," says McKeil.

It's all part of a remarkable journey that began more than 40 years ago when Blair McKeil's father, Evans McKeil, founded the Hamilton-based company.

For Evans McKeil, the business was in his blood. As a youngster in Pugwash, Nova Scotia in the 1930s, he watched boats head out to sea from this fishing port of 600 souls. His uncles sailed cargo-laden schooners across the Bay of Fundy to St. John, N.B. And, following the Second World War, a teenaged Evans McKeil helped his father, lumber mill owner William McKeil, build a few boats.

So it's not surprising this transplanted blue-noser is today chairman of McKeil Marine, operating the largest tugboat and barge fleet on the Great Lakes.

In 1948, a languishing Maritime economy convinced Evans McKeil's parents to head for prosperous Hamilton – and he followed a year later.

> "We're diversifying our services, filling niche markets that tugs and barges were previously not used in."

Evans McKeil joined the former McNamara Marine Co. in 1950, performing dredging and constructing bridges, wharves and locks. Then, in the fall of 1955 came a fateful suggestion from a Newfoundland skipper familiar with the McKeil family background.

"He said I should work for myself and build my own boats," recalls McKeil, 67, "so I rented a barn in Ancaster and built a 35-foot-long workboat – the MicMac."

The all-wood MicMac was launched from Hamilton Harbour Commissioners' docks at the foot of James Street North in the spring. This 1956 launch marked the founding of McKeil Marine.

Powered by a six cylinder Chevy car engine, the MicMac was put to work by McKeil Marine transporting work crews building the St. Lawrence Seaway system.

McKeil Marine does everything from ferrying crews at Newfoundland's Hibernia project to docking boats at Hamilton Harbour.

Although he later sold the MicMac to a friend, McKeil continued to build up a fleet of purchased used boats which by the late 1950s numbered 10 tugs plus barges.

In the early 1960s, McKeil was joined by his master mechanic brother, Doug McKeil, who fixed boats bought from the Royal Canadian Navy and other sources.

McKeil Marine is truly a family based firm. Evans McKeil, his wife Florence and their two sons, Blair and Garth, all play a major role in day-to-day operations. The company employs many other family members in various positions including superintendents, captains, engineers, deckhands and general manager.

Blair McKeil was named president in 1992 and became responsible for overseeing all company operations. Under his leadership, McKeil Marine has experienced continuous growth and now boasts over 100 full-time employees and a fleet in excess of 100 tugs and barges.

"The main contributing factor to our success is our people," asserts McKeil. "Their open attitudes and eagerness to succeed have enabled us to try new things, learn and move forward. I guess you could say we are all growing and learning together. Each day is a new adventure."

Within the McKeil fleet, there are a variety of tugs ranging in size from small workboats to large ocean-going tugs and supply boats. The barge fleet includes small, portable barges used for inland projects to large ocean-going barges too large to transit the St. Lawrence Seaway.

Today, McKeil Marine has equipment working throughout the Great Lakes, the St. Lawrence River, the Maritimes, Newfoundland, Northern Labrador and Europe. "On any given day," notes McKeil, "you can have a large flat deck barge loading pulpwood in Goose Bay, Labrador, a tank unloading oil in Quebec City, or a large barge being beached in Voisey Bay to unload a camp."

"At the same time, our tugs are docking ships in Hamilton, Toronto and Port Weller – and a McKeil ferry is moving tractor trailers between Windsor and Detroit," he adds.

"Our future depends on our ability to continually find new markets for growth – while at the same time providing excellent service to our repeat customers."

▶
*As president, Blair McKeil continues to steer McKeil Marine in the right direction.*
*– PHOTO BY DAVID GRUGGEN*

# McKeil Marine

*Success* 43 *Stories*

# Hamilton Harbour Commissioners

A massive freighter unloads iron ore at Dofasco's steel mill docks at Hamilton Harbour. Further west, McKeil Marine tugboats push a barge eastward, en route to Montreal.

Westward still, the harbour becomes a recreational paradise with sailboats and pleasure craft skimming across calm blue waters lined by a lush green shoreline.

It's just another day in Canada's Heartland Harbour.

While some Great Lakes harbours are in decline, Hamilton's is prospering. And a primary reason for Hamilton Harbour's success is its diversity of strengths, asserts Bob Hennessy, port director of the Hamilton Harbour Commissioners which has administered the harbour since 1912 under an act of federal parliament.

HHC is a self-sufficient agency which is not government-funded, but instead derives its revenue from shipping, docking and other fees.

"This is a multi-faceted harbour with recreation, shipping, industry and natural environment all co-existing and complementing one another," explains Hennessy, whose James Street North offices offer a sweeping view the harbour.

"Now, more than ever before, this is where it all comes together."

Hennessy notes today's balance follows a tortured evolution in which the harbour went from being a purely natural setting to a recreational area and then to a primarily industrial area.

"In the past, each one of the harbour's personalities was at odds with the others, often to the point of detrimentally affecting the others," points out Hennessy, an eighth-generation Canadian who enjoys the Great Outdoors, especially the natural areas of the harbour. HHC owns 500 acres plus 6,000 acres under water.

"Today, industry is heavily involved in environmental improvements," notes Jeff Brookfield, HHC port planner and BAIT (Bay Area Implementation Team) member.

"The region has built several sewage holding tanks which have virtually eliminated untreated sewage from entering the harbour, and the water quality has improved tremendously as a result," adds Brookfield, noting that natural weedbeds and fish stock are making an impressive comeback. "Recreational use of the harbour is greater now than it's ever been, in part because of Pier Four Park and the creation of Bayfront Park from the former Lax industrial lands," he adds.

Enrolment is up at the HHC's Sailing and Powerboating School, credited with offering Ontario's finest sailing program. And there are the nearby world-class amenities offered by the Royal Hamilton Yacht Club, Leander Boat Club and the Harbour West Marina Complex.

Adding to the harbour's recreational experience are Fisherman's Pier, Eastport ship viewing parkette and, on the naturally forested Burlington side, LaSalle Park.

> "This a multi-faceted harbour with recreation, shipping, industry and natural environment all co-existing."

There are also timely improvements taking place in the harbour's industrial lands, after years of industrial downsizing and dislocation, which resulted in reduced employment at the steel mills and led to the loss of major employers such as Otis Elevator and International Harvester.

HHC acquired 100 acres of Pier 15 lands, formerly owned by International Harvester, turning it into a light industrial park, leasing space to over 20 companies, including McKeil Marine, sandblasting and granulated materials firm Bell & Mackenzie and S&B Food Equipment.

And this business park, west from the foot of Sherman Avenue North, also features De Feo Auto Service, the city's best-kept secret for reasonably priced, expert auto repairs.

"I know it looks rough," owner-president Sergio De Feo says of his industrial surroundings, "but the rent is low, so we're keeping our costs down and passing the savings on to our customers."

The success of De Feo and others in this informal industrial park, is evidence of the HHC achieving its own success, revitalizing once-vacant lands to allow entrepreneurs to act on their ideas.

Reduced steel-related tonnage from shifts in the global marketplace has been somewhat offset by growth in shipments of liquid, bulk and agricultural products.

This includes tonnage from Hamilton's CanAmera Foods, the largest oil seed crushing plant in Eastern Canada. As well, about 25 per cent of Welland Canal tonnage ends up at Hamilton Harbour.

"Most other ports on the Great Lakes are doing a lot less business," notes Fred Rose, the HHC's manager of trade and development. "We've held our own – even grown a bit," he adds.

"We're one of the most consistently profitable ports in Canada. Our cargo rates haven't gone up since 1990 so our revenue growth is from new business."

HHC revenue in 1996 approached $11 million while profit topped $2.2 million with much of this sum reinvested in port facilities. Total shipments in 1996 rose to nearly 13 million tonnes, up from 11.9 million tonnes the year before.

Beyond diversification, much of HHC's success stems from a willingness – make that a determination – to eliminate as much delay as possible.

"Several years ago, we had some business people come up here from Houston, Texas, to set up some agricultural product tanks," recalls Hennessy. "They went home the same day with all the approvals they needed. They were amazed it could all be done in a few hours. There is no red tape here – that's a non-starter."

Hennessy expresses confidence that HHC staff will continue to achieve new levels of success by ensuring a can-do attitude remains at its warehouses, dockyards and other facilities.

It seems to be working: Much of the HHC's modern day growth has come from referrals and from the growing needs of successful tenants.

"We have to stay customer-focused," says Hennessy, "because if we ever stop, we won't be here any longer."

"Our role," he adds, "is to continue developing the harbour in ways that best serve our customers and our community."

▶

*While some Great Lakes harbours are in decline, Hamilton Harbour is prospering. A true success story, the harbour is one of the busiest port facilities in Canada.*

# Hamilton Harbour Commissioners

*Success* 45 *Stories*

– PHOTO BY DAVID GRUGGEN

# CHAPTER 4

# Financial Advisors

# Financial Advisors

Thinking of making an investment, establishing an RRSP, taking out a mortgage?

Chances are you've already used the services of a financial planner, mortgage broker or other form of financial advisor.

And we'll all be turning to financial advisors more frequently in the years ahead as our aging population struggles to get the best deal possible on a mortgage, tap into the most promising investment returns and achieve a degree of financial independence before we retire.

As we age, there's a growing acceptance – however reluctant – of our own mortality, coupled with the need to take steps today to ensure tomorrow doesn't hold a life of poverty. There's also a growing realization government pensions and programs may fall far short of meeting our actual needs and expectations.

We need to take measures now to independently see to our future needs.

As more and more Canadians focus on building wealth, increasing numbers of us are turning to the experts to help us make the right decisions and investments.

And all of this is generating burgeoning growth in the financial services sector.

"Financial management services represent an absolutely huge industry," says Neil Everson, manager of business development for the Hamilton-Wentworth Economic Development Department.

"The baby boomers are not only generating great wealth – they're inheriting wealth as well," notes Everson, citing studies which indicate Canada's baby boom generation will inherit over $2 trillion in passed-on wealth.

David Foot, author of Boom, Bust & Echo, suggests the Baby Boomers will come to dominate the financial sector just as they forever changed and shaped the course of society, music, entertainment and other facets of life.

Foot believes baby boomers collectively caused the real estate boom of the late 1980s and in the late 1990s followed that up by successfully creating a sustained stock market boom.

Low interest rates leave this aging population to find other ways of realizing a significant return on money invested for retirement. More often than not, the chosen vehicle consists of stocks-based mutual funds tucked away into Registered Retirement Savings Plans. The resulting burgeoning growth in RRSP-held mutual funds has driven up stock prices and generated new record levels of investment.

"Just 15 years ago, hardly anyone was investing in mutual funds," notes Lee Kirkby, the former executive director of the Hamilton and District Chamber of Commerce.

"Back then, mutual funds seemed to be confined to the very wealthy," Kirkby continues. "Today, mutual funds are virtually a commodity – and everyone seems to be investing in them."

And, the average consumer is evolving into a sophisticated investor who shops very carefully for mutual funds and financial advisors. RRSPs and investments have become hot topics.

Kirkby points to a growing public interest in how investments are made and how funds are managed.

"All you have to do is check out a retirement planning seminar," he observes, "and you'll find hundreds of people in attendance. It wasn't long ago that such seminars would be sparsely attended. But that's changed now. There's a realization that planning for retirement is extremely important to people, and that's a healthy development."

Another development – which isn't particularly healthy – is a societal shift to busier, more complicated lives.

Downsized companies demand much more from multi-skilled, computer-literate workforces. Longer work days are the norm, as are two-income families, who juggle work, social and family commitments in an often futile attempt to recapture a lifestyle once possible with a single income. Too many of us are running on a treadmill, in a perpetual state of exhaustion chasing the Canadian dream. We have our hands full with the demands of daily living.

Who has time to monitor investments, engineer financial independence or map out a retirement strategy?

A rapidly growing number of Canadians are turning to the experts for assistance in capturing the best mortgage deal, the right investments, the most effective approach to achieving, first financial security, then financial independence.

"The enormous growth of the financial planning services sector," Kirkby says, "is in large part a response to specialization."

"As things become more complicated, there's a realization it's all becoming too much to deal with on our own. That's when we tend to turn to financial experts to help build our wealth and our pensions while we concentrate on the things we do best."

One expert increasing numbers of people are turning to is Armando Vacca, president of A. D. Vacca and Associates, Financial Planning Group.

My wife, Philippa, and I were fortunate that we turned to Vacca after I engineered a dramatic career change, leaving The Spectator after 17 years to begin a new life as a freelance writer and author of business books.

Caught up in writing Success Stories, I didn't take the time to question the effectiveness of my investments, the adequacy of my insurance coverage, the financial needs of my family.

Vacca guided my wife and I through a comprehensive financial planning process which resulted in our switching to investments with growth records in tune with our future retirement needs. Our insurance was increased and our financial security was enhanced.

We're now in much better financial shape, thanks to Vacca's holistic approach towards building financial independence.

Another expert drawing a growing following is Rainer Puder, president of Mortgage Advantage, who provides advice on managing household expenses and can arrange mortgages at lower interest rates than his clients could attain on their own.

> "Average consumers are evolving into sophisticated investors who shop carefully for mutual funds and financial advisors."

# Financial Advisors

*Mortgage broker Rainer Puder discusses various mortgage options with author Michael B. Davie and his wife Philippa.*
*– PHOTO BY DAVID GRUGGEN*

Puder also sat down with my wife and I to guide us through a range of mortgage options from a number of financial institutions. Through this process, we were able to find a low-interest, flexible-terms mortgage which best suited our needs.

This skilful mortgage broker is also equally adept at securing mortgages for people who might otherwise fail to qualify.

He's made the dream of home ownership a reality for many struggling couples who are now happily building equity – and residing in – their biggest single asset.

Puder's ability to negotiate the lowest mortgage rates possible for more financially secure couples provides many advantages. These clients benefit from lower carrying costs, freeing up more disposable income, which can then be invested or used to pay down the mortgage. His services have become an important part of many couples' plans for financial success.

Jerry Santucci, a financial planner with Berkshire Investment Group Inc., has modelled his investing approach after one of the world's richest investors, Warren Buffett.

Santucci is also building a following with his effective, go-slow approach to investing and his wise counsel to buy the stock of good companies and hang onto it as long as possible.

All of these financial advisors are listed in the directory at the back of this book for research purposes and ready reference.

We'll now take a closer look at the success stories of Vacca, Puder and Santucci in the ensuing series of profiles.

*Success Stories*

# A.D. Vacca & Associates

Armando David Vacca was still in his late teens when his father died suddenly of a heart attack.

The 1976 death of Pasqualino Vacca left his family in emotional and financial chaos. He had been a seemingly healthy, dependable steelworker with over 20 years service at Stelco Inc. His heart stopped in his mid-40s due to blood-clotting complications from back surgery.

"My family really wasn't prepared at all for this event or the future," recalls Armando Vacca, now 40.

The unexpected death would prove a turning point in Armando Vacca's life.

At age 19, when most of his peers were enjoying carefree lives, Vacca found himself growing up fast, sorting out the complexities of his family's finances and future needs. He remembers it as an intensive learning experience – and it would profoundly change his life.

"I was motivated to bring about some kind of security for my family," Vacca says, "and I didn't want to see other families go through this kind of chaos. Out of that tragedy came a sense of purpose."

"My own family was unprepared for the future and, over time, I found other good, honest people similarly unprepared. The realization that these problems existed catapulted me into financial planning. I had found my mission in life."

With his focus firmly on the financial, and a desire to achieve his own degree of security, Vacca enrolled in the three-year Business Administration program at Mohawk College, graduating in 1980 on the Deans' Honour List.

He became licensed to sell life and disability insurance and mutual funds. And he went into financial planning, starting Money Concepts (Stoney Creek) in 1988.

Vacca, CFP, RFP (Certified Financial Planner and Registered Financial Planner), now heads up Hamilton-based A.D. Vacca & Associates, Financial Planning Group.

With a support staff of five, the fee and commission-based financial planner manages over $40 million in assets on behalf of his clients, from his expanded offices at Queenston Road in the city's east end.

He is also president of the Hamilton-Niagara Chapter of CAFP (Canadian Association of Financial Planners), fostering professionalism and high ethical standards. And he's a member of CAPP (Canadian Association of Pre-retirement Planners) and IAFP (International Association for Financial Planning).

By 1982, the advent of the personal computer meant that financial plans which once took five to seven days to prepare could now be assembled in five to seven hours. The change meant that financial planning, once a luxury confined to the very wealthy, was now affordable for middle income Canadians.

> "As more companies downsize, rightsize and capsize, more people will turn to financial planners for advice."

"We're offering financial planning for the unchauffered and yachtless," smiles Vacca, who has broadened his client base to help families of ordinary means achieve financial security and independence.

Less affluent couples have benefitted from his advice, turning their lives around to achieve success. And success, by Vacca's definition, includes much more than financial wealth.

Offering what is essentially one-stop financial planning solutions for families, he examines each client's interrelationship between their money and work life, their family and social life and their health and spiritual well-being.

"Each one of the areas in this triangle of life impacts on all the others and can affect the ultimate goal of financial independence," explains Vacca, in an interview at his office.

"If your financial situation is problematic, it doesn't take long before there is also a strain on your family life," notes Vacca as he busily sketches an illustration of the three-way dynamic.

"And if your family or social life is in turmoil, it's not long before it affects productivity at work – and has you losing sleep at night," he adds.

By focusing on financial and other sides of the three-sided equation, Vacca's rare – but effective – holistic approach provides a compelling and complete picture of a client's state of life.

Utilizing reference point financial planning techniques, Vacca helps clients set up short-term goals, including advanced cash management strategies which maximize the effectiveness of limited cash resources. Also established are mid-term goals, including strategic investment and tax design for children's education; retirement and estate planning.

Next, he helps establish a priority placement of goals on behalf of the client – or clients, as couples are treated as teams jointly searching for mutually agreeable solutions.

Key to this process is personal risk management, including achieving the right levels of house, car disability, life and health insurance protection against a potential loss of income of assets.

Continuing this process of illumination, Vacca assists in restructuring debts; using debt to advantage; and sometimes pooling borrowed sums into a single, low-interest loan, freeing up money which can then be invested with higher return rates while saving taxes and enhancing lifestyle.

"Many people feel they have to have a lot of money to become involved in financial planning," Vacca observes.

"But it's quite possible to achieve a good deal of financial success with two incomes which together gross $50,000," he explains. "And I can take someone with less income than that and help them achieve financial success in their life."

Vacca guides his clients through a maze of mutual funds, bypassing many of the 1,600 funds on the market to find the right mix of investments among 150 of the better funds. Investing is strongly influenced by the client's comfort with levels of risk, investment needs, affordability and an intent to maintain or improve existing lifestyles in the process.

"It's important to find the right balance of investment growth and risk for the client," says Vacca who likens this exercise to driving from Hamilton to Toronto.

Driving slowly may reduce the risk but it can take too long to get where you want to go. Speeding may get you there faster, but it also carries higher risks (accidents,

# A.D. Vacca & Associates

*Financial planner Armando Vacca has achieved personal success by helping others achieve financial success.*
– PHOTO BY DAVID GRUGGEN

speeding tickets) that can prove harmful, he explains, adding that risk and gain are balanced if you drive at the speed limit.

Many people in the financial services sector emphasize a particular product, he notes, whether it's an investment, tax preparation, insurance or banking.

Full service financial planners such as Vacca offer expertise in all of these areas, helping the client build a blueprint for financial independence and success based on all of their life needs and aspirations.

It's a role he sees increasing as more Canadians find themselves on their own, without a traditional, paternalistic employer to see to their overall financial needs.

"Ten years ago, 7 per cent of the population was self-employed. Today, anywhere from 15-18 per cent of the population has taken the entrepreneurial leap, going from dependency to interdependency," he says.

"As more companies downsize, rightsize and capsize, more people will turn to financial planners for advice – and I'm looking forward to helping them as much as possible."

*Success Stories*

# Mortgage Advantage

For too many Canadians, the dream of home ownership remains just that: A dream.

No matter how far mortgage rates fall, these would-be homeowners can't seem to get their finances in order.

They're often deemed uncreditworthy and rejected for loans.

For others, more financially solid, moving to a larger home can be forever delayed when mortgage rates stubbornly resist falling enough for them to comfortably take on a larger mortgage.

Rainer Puder enjoys making new home dreams come true for both groups.

As broker/consultant of Hamilton-based Mortgage Advantage Corp., Puder routinely assists the second group of home buyers by getting them mortgage rates half a percentage point or more below the lender's published rates.

His negotiating power comes in part from the volume of business Mortgage Advantage brings the lenders. The firm generates millions of dollars annually in pre-screened mortgage deals. Lenders are only too happy to pay Puder a finder's fee and pass on a rate break to the consumer.

Along with agents Gordon Marr and Frank Despond, Puder also eagerly aids many clients in the first group, those who have previously been turned down for a mortgage. Although he still has to turn away some would-be clients who are simply too great a credit risk, he is able to help impressive numbers of people once rejected by lenders.

"I feel successful when people think of us as an instrument that helped them achieve home ownership or rectify a bad financial situation," says Puder, whose Upper James Street office, south of Mohawk Road, also employs his wife Linda as receptionist and office manager.

As the first company representative many clients encounter, she plays a vital role in the firm's success.

Rainer Puder meets with these less financially secure clients – usually in their home – scrutinizes their finances and then addresses issues of their existing debtload, income sources and future prospects.

He's often successful in obtaining a mortgage either through the banks and trust companies, finance companies, private lenders or a combination of these.

Since lenders won't pay a finder's fee for these deals, he assesses these clients a modest broker fee when he succeeds in getting them a mortgage they'd otherwise never attain. The work provides a strong sense of satisfaction.

"Basically, I like helping people," says Puder. "I do listen and I do understand," he explains. "If you do something good for someone, they'll tell 10 friends. Do something bad, they'll tell 20."

It's a balancing act: Puder also takes seriously his obligation to the lenders.

> *If you're in business for yourself, there's a lot of pressure to succeed. To me, success is surviving under your own power.*

"I also have to keep lenders happy – I can't expose them to unreasonable risk," asserts Puder, comfortably ensconced behind his desk at second-floor offices with an inviting homey atmosphere and Victorian decor.

"I'll present my client's case in the best possible light, without in any way clouding over risks or misrepresenting a situation – the lender has to be told the good, the bad and the ugly," adds Puder, whose lenders include TD Bank, Mutual Life, Montreal Trust, Beneficial Finance and National Bank.

Rainer Puder and Mortgage advantage have earned a reputation for honest, detailed risk assessments, making the job of the lenders that much easier.

His recommendation is often enough to secure mortgage deals the lenders might otherwise walk away from.

It's a role that's at odds with the historically unfavourable – and today, undeserved – view of mortgage brokers.

Unlike loan brokers, mortgage brokers are required to be licensed, and registered. They're also regulated and are subject to periodic business audits. "I'm proud to say I'm a mortgage broker assisting both the client and the lender – but I'm the go-between, nothing more," Puder points out.

A growing number of real estate sales people are happily letting this "go-between" and his associates go to bat for their clients, securing their mortgages or capturing rate discounts, making real estate deals happen in the process.

Mortgage Advantage has tripled its volume since opening for business in 1994. Yet the company would never have been formed if not for a catastrophic moment in this mortgage broker's life.

A once-secure banker earning $60,000 a year, Puder was downsized out of a job in 1991 when the National Bank of Canada closed his department.

"At first I couldn't believe it had happened. You think you have some security – but there's no security today."

After taking on some menial jobs, Puder rejoined the financial sector in 1992, first as manager of mortgage services for Royal Trust, and later as an agent for Mortgage Financial Corp.

By spring of 1994, having successfully endured employment upheaval, Puder was ready to act on a dream of running his own business. Mortgage Advantage was born, financed by cashed-in RRSPs and a New Venture Loan. "I realized I could do a lot better on my own," Puder states. "Now I make the decisions."

He's also retained a healthy degree of sympathy and understanding for struggling couples. He knows what it's like to face job loss and an uncertain financial future: He's been there.

To others attempting to achieve success by going into business for themselves, Puder advises perseverance, keeping your word, earning a reputation for honesty, working hard and being as helpful as possible to your clients.

"If you're in business for yourself – either through choice or circumstances – there's a lot of pressure to succeed. Even more so, if you start out with little financial backing," he says. "To me, success is surviving under your own power and helping others in the process."

▶
*Rainer Puder, with three of the people who stand behind him: Frank Despond, Linda Puder and Gordon Marr.*
– PHOTO BY DAVID GRUGGEN

*Success Stories*

# Mortgage Advantage

## Success 53 Stories

# Jerry Santucci

When it comes to building wealth, it's hard to fault Jerry Santucci's choice of role model.

Santucci, financial advisor and wealth management specialist with Berkshire Investment Group, draws his inspiration from billionaire investor Warren Buffett.

Ranked by Forbes magazine as the third-richest American, Buffett differs from others on the Forbes list as all his wealth was built from investing, not from owning a successful company.

Buffett's 1993 net worth of $8 billion (US) had nearly tripled by 1997 to $23.2 billion (US) held by Berkshire Hathaway, a former textiles firm he had bought and turned into his holding company.

"Buffett is the richest investor of all time, he's our role model and we study his recipe for success," stresses Santucci, of Berkshire Securities at the Burlington office of Berkshire Group. The company derives its name – and inspiration – from Buffett's holding company, although there is no affiliation of any kind.

What are the ingredients to the Buffett recipe? "Well," Santucci says thoughtfully, "first you should acquire an ownership stake in outstanding, well-managed companies in growth industries."

"Then, hold onto it for a very long time," adds Santucci, in an interview at his North Service Road, Burlington office. "Buffett's own favourite investment time span is forever. That way, you defer taxes on your investment and it keeps growing."

Further criteria, adds Santucci, includes never buying into a company whose products or services you don't understand.

You should also avoid cyclical or resource-based companies and stick with proven earners with strong balance sheets and a history of consistent predictable earnings and cash flow.

Santucci, 40, recommends money managers in different countries who closely follow Buffett's long-term investment approach. For Canadian investments, Santucci promotes AIC Mutual Funds which are known for buying shares in financial services companies.

Chairman Michael Lee-Chin has turned AIC into a powerful mutual fund company. While affiliated with AIC, Berkshire is an independent dealer with over 40 offices across the nation, and a network of 170 sales representatives.

"We use Buffett as the model and by applying his criteria, we eliminate most of the investments out there, to concentrate on the investing in the best companies around," explains Santucci, who shops the market on behalf of a clientele of over 250 individuals and groups.

One of Berkshire's elite, top-performing Gold Circle Club members, Santucci became intrigued at an early age with the dynamics of successful investing.

Santucci, who grew up in Hamilton and now resides in Burlington, earned a BA in economics from Western University at London, Ontario.

> "Buffett is the richest investor of all time, he's our role model and we study his recipe for success."

In 1983, he joined the Investors Group and became a successful financial advisor and seller of mutual funds. The funds can contain everything from stocks to bonds, Guaranteed Investment Certificates and other forms of investment. Santucci left Investors in 1992 to join Berkshire where he's licensed to sell mutual funds, insurance, securities and tax shelters.

Santucci soon furthered his reputation as a conscientious financial advisor who builds investment portfolios based on each client's needs and risk comfort level. He currently has over $40 million in assets under his administration.

Santucci employs a thorough approach which includes collecting the client's financial and personal data, determining their goals and commitments, explaining investment philosophy and then making investment recommendations.

He acts as a guide, navigating the client into the right investment streams in a mutual funds industry that has grown from $4 billion in the early 1980s to $280 billion in the fall of 1997.

"There's a proliferation of products out there – I try to cut through the confusion and create an investment strategy that's right for the client," he explains.

Although many people still rely on well-meaning friends and relatives for free financial advice, Santucci suggests that using non-experts for investment advice often only creates the illusion of savings.

"The real cost of this advice is that you can end up with bad investments or a much lower return than you might achieve if you listened instead to an advisor who bases his advice on the investment approach of someone like Buffett, who has earned billions of dollars."

Santucci warns against placing too much emphasis on a newspaper's stocks page as it's really just a financial scoreboard which provides little indication of a firm's investment potential.

"When you go to a football game, you pay attention to what's happening on the field, you don't spend all your time staring at the scoreboard. It's much the same with companies. What's most important is their operations, their business strategy, not their daily stock price listings."

Santucci also advises keeping your cool when stock prices suddenly dip.

"Such corrections in the market happen periodically for any number of reasons, most of which have little to do with a company's performance. In the short term stock prices often don't match a company's earnings. But longer term – five to 10 years – they do tend to match."

And the returns can be considerable. Santucci notes that a $100,000 bungalow purchased 10 years ago would only be worth $150,000 to $170,000 today. However, $100,000 worth of Coca Cola shares purchased a decade ago are today worth $1.4 million.

The most effective way to achieve investment growth is to take a measured, long-term approach to wealth creation, Santucci advises.

"I like to follow Buffett's practice of buying the best companies and holding onto their stock as long as possible. I believe in taking a patient, disciplined approach to investing. There's nothing wrong with getting rich slowly."

▶

*Taking a patient approach to investing, Jerry Santucci draws his inspiration from billionaire investor Warren Buffett.*
– PHOTO BY DAVID GRUGGEN

#  *Jerry Santucci*

*Success* 55 *Stories*

– *PHOTO BY DAVID GRUGGEN*

# CHAPTER 5

# *The Entrepreneurs*

# The Entrepreneurs

What is it that makes a successful entrepreneur? A creative spark? An all-consuming passion? Perseverance and determination? Lee Kirkby ponders the question for a moment.

"In some cases it's probably one or two of these characteristics – in most cases it's likely a combination of all of them," answers Kirkby, the former executive director of the Hamilton and District Chamber of Commerce.

"Successful business people I've talked to often refer to a business idea and a business focus which together become an all-consuming passion, driving them to achieve success," observes Kirkby, who served eight years as executive director before accepting a position in 1997 as vice-president of advanced products, and manager of the document imaging department at Leppert Business Equipment.

"They're able to place a commanding focus on what they're trying to do," he adds, "and they're able to identify opportunities and respond to them in a timely manner."

Unfortunately, even the brightest ideas and greatest efforts can end in failure, as the collapse of so many start-up businesses indicates. Often, all that is needed is a little more time to generate sufficient cash flow. Or there's a need for some expert advice to resolve business problems before they become life-threatening to a young enterprise.

To help fledgling entrepreneurs survive and thrive through those early make-it-or-break-it years, Hamilton-Wentworth region built and sponsors GHTEC (Greater Hamilton Technology Enterprise Centre,) which acts as an incubator for start-up firms, particularly in such sectors as automotive parts, advanced materials, telecommunications, medical devices, food processing or environmental services.

These business tenants effectively manage their costs by sharing secretaries, receptionists, telephone answering services, typing services, photo copiers, fax machines, computer equipment, library resource centre, seminars, meeting rooms and other amenities with their fellow entrepreneurial tenants at GHTEC which is operated by the BAC (Business Advisory Centre).

But the biggest advantage enjoyed by GHTEC (pronounced Gee-Tek) tenants is access to expert know-how through mentoring programs which, for nominal fees, bring new business people in contact with over 200 experienced specialists from all areas of business. On loan from 30 large Hamilton-area firms, they provide invaluable, timely technical and business-oriented advice.

The $4 million, 40,000-square-foot GHTEC facility has already given a healthy head start to several thousand clients, including Patrick Whyte and Alistair Davie (no relation to the author), the founders of Comtek Advanced Structures, which began as a two-man company and now employs 36 people in the field of repairing composite aircraft components.

Operating and driving GHTEC's services and programs is the BAC itself, a non-profit organization, founded in 1977 by senior members of Dofasco, Stelco, Westinghouse Canada and other companies who recognized a need to assist small to mid-sized enterprises resolve technical or management programs.

"I wish there had been something like GHTEC around when we started our company in 1973," says Dr. Wally Pieczonka, BAC chairman and chairman and founder of Burlington-based Linear Technology, now known as Gennum Corporation, a major manufacturer of circuitry and hearing instrument components.

"There's no single solution to our economic problems," asserts Pieczonka, who feels the best approach is to "take a lot of small ideas and build on them."

The cumulative effect of such an approach leads to large benefits. Statistics routinely show that the bulk of Canadians aren't employed by large corporations. Instead, much of the working population is employed by small firms which each boast only a few jobs, but collectively employ millions of people.

> *"We have to help those who are entrepreneurial by providing them with the knowledge and information they need to attain success."*

"One firm hiring 1,000 people may grab the headlines," notes BAC president and CEO Ron Wallace. "But 1,000 firms each hiring one person is just as effective and has just as much economic impact."

Wallace points out that the BAC is the economic equivalent of a recreation centre "and most communities don't have a BAC – but wish they did."

"If we want an economy that's a winner, he says, "we have to help those who are entrepreneurial in nature by providing them with the knowledge and information they need to attain their own degree of success."

"The BAC is playing a crucial role in helping entrepreneurs to help themselves," explains Wallace.

"If we want an entrepreneurial society, then we need the BAC to share information and help develop new entrepreneurs. We're in an unforgiving economic environment," he adds.

"Many new firms can't afford to learn by their mistakes because their mistakes could finish them off before they really get their business started."

One advantage of helping more small firms succeed is that they tend to grow in size. And even when they're still small, their sheer numbers have a very beneficial impact on employment.

Another advantage is that these companies help larger firms prosper by becoming their dependable customers or suppliers, creating another snowballing economic benefit.

"It's vitally important that we have local firms that sell and buy from each other," asserts Wallace, who joined the BAC as its executive director in 1991 after spending 35 years with Westinghouse Canada.

Self confidence is also vitally important if entrepreneurs are to succeed, adds Wallace.

"Americans are very good at selling themselves, sometimes even beyond what they're capable of actually delivering" notes Wallace, adding that "generally speaking, Canadians are competent while Americans are confident."

# The Entrepreneurs

*The Greater Hamilton Technology Centre, built and sponsored by Hamilton-Wentworth region, helps fledgling entrepreneurs survive and thrive through the early make-it-or-break-it years.*
– PHOTO BY DENNIS MCGREAL

But this shouldn't be interpreted as a compliment, Wallace warns. "If you think being modest will win you an order, believe me, it won't. We have to be more aggressive and confident based on our own competence."

Wallace says entrepreneurs can more easily be successful if they begin their business with proven competence in a given field, a strong reason to start a business, a clear understanding of what they're getting into and a knowledge base built on one to two years of research and attending seminars on starting a business.

Studies have indicated that future generations of Canadians will be working for companies that don't exist today.

"If you want to know where the jobs will be coming from in the future," says Wallace, "you can be relatively certain a lot of the jobs will be created by entrepreneurs."

"Entrepreneurs and self-employment are the way of the future, agrees Sandie Heirwegh, manager of the BAC's Entrepreneurial Program. Heirwegh points to studies predicting that by the year 2000 some 40 per cent of all of the workers in Canada will be self-employed, busily working at their own companies.

And 90 per cent of these new companies will have fewer than five employees, adds Heirwegh, whose program breaks from a structured classroom model. It instead provides coaching and consultation help to entrepreneurs who use this assistance to look at alternatives before formulating their own business strategies.

*Success Stories*

# The Entrepreneurs

**D**riving, at least partly, a trend to self-employment and entrepreneurialism is ongoing employment upheaval and downsizing by traditional major employers.

"Job displacement certainly continues to be a major reason," says Heirwegh, noting that as companies shed workers, some of the displaced employees are able to recover from the devastation of job loss and turn this disadvantage into a new opportunity.

"We're seeing a number of people who have lost their jobs and decided to seize the opportunity to go into business on their own," she asserts. "Some of those displaced workers see self-employment as a chance to earn what they feel they're really worth."

But Heirwegh also observes another, growing, phenomenon fuelling entrepreneurialism. "Self-employment was once considered a viable alternative out of necessity, due to job loss," Heirwegh explains. "Now we're seeing more and more people turning to self-employment for another reason. It's being seen as a viable alternative out of desire, not necessity."

In fact, Heirwegh cites desire for success as the leading reason for new business start-ups. "People want to be their own boss these days," she notes. "They're tired of placing their future in somebody else's hands. They want to take control of their own destiny. That's the biggest reason for people to launch their business. And it's why we're here: To help them."

"We're seeing people leaving jobs simply because they want to go out on their own and are confident they can achieve greater success on their own," she adds. "They're confident of making it on their own – and they often succeed."

The BAC itself is filled with success stories. From its April 1993 founding to the fall of 1997, the BAC has had 900 people go through its Entrepreneurial Program to start a business.

Normally, four out of five new businesses fail in their first year of operation. The BAC has reversed this trend: Fully 75-80 per cent of its graduate businesses are still operating.

"We have many entrepreneurs who started small and got big," notes Heirwegh. "But whether they're big or small, they share a common desire and determination to succeed – and, of course, these business share an entrepreneurial streak."

That entrepreneurial streak appears to be a potent combination of creativity, persistence and willingness to risk everything to see an idea succeed.

Kirkby has found, not surprisingly, that many business leaders he's encountered possess various entrepreneurial attributes.

"That little creative spark I admire is in a lot of people I come across but how successful they are often depends on how well they can translate their idea into a viable business," he explains. "But I see positive, unique entrepreneurial characteristics in many people in and out of the chamber."

Kirkby cites other entrepreneurial hallmarks, including tenacity, marketing flair and brilliance, a charismatic presence, people skills, an ability to find and exploit market opportunities and a single-mindedness towards building a business.

"Often with limited assets, the successful entrepreneur can take an idea and springboard it into something wonderful," Kirby enthuses. "And they achieve success financially and in other ways by meeting and exceeding expectations."

"When they decide something will be successful – it's hard to tell them otherwise," says Kirkby, who declines mentioning names to this point. "And they'll just bulldoze ahead," he adds, while noting "that quality can be both a positive and a negative – but there's no question it generates the drive and momentum needed to seize an opportunity."

Pressed for examples of hard-driving entrepreneurs, Kirkby catches his breath, then names a couple of prominent business leaders: billionaire businessman Michael DeGroote and Vineland Estates president and proprietor John Howard.

"What I find so impressive about Mike DeGroote is that he was able to achieve enormous success in such different areas," Kirkby says. "He started out in trucking, then went into school buses, then into waste management, and now he's involved in a big way in insurance companies – and he's achieving great success there too."

"John Howard also amazes me for much the same reason," Kirkby confides.

"Here's a guy who made it big selling photocopiers and he was somehow able to translate this success into a successful winery and restaurant business. He's a marketing genius who succeeds in entirely different fields," explains Kirkby. "Whether this quality is taught or innate depends on the individual."

I'm not about to argue with Kirkby's assessment of either of these remarkable gentleman. Having known them both for a number of years, I too am still somewhat awe-struck by their business prowess and creativity, their drive, self-confidence and sheer ability to succeed at whatever they put their minds to.

John Howard's most admirable traits may be his ability to bring out the best in people and his insistence on giving credit to others. Yes, he purchased a successful Ontario vineyard and winery from the Weis family of gifted winemakers from Germany's Mosel Valley. But Howard has added much more to this equation.

Howard's Vineland Estates property now boasts a superb restaurant, a cozy banquet hall from a restored carriage house, a bed and breakfast establishment, and, of course, many new and exciting wines.

And, it's hard not to be impressed by Michael DeGroote's approach to business. Early on, he failed in business, declaring personal and business bankruptcy.

Although he was not required to do so by law, DeGroote spent years making sure every creditor was repaid. He refused to let insolvency stand in the way of honouring every commitment.

He proved his word is better than any written contract.

> *"Often, with limited assets, the successful entrepreneur can take an idea and springboard it into something wonderful."*

# The Entrepreneurs

*In a light-hearted moment at home, Michael G. DeGroote joins his 'brother George' at the piano. The billionaire businessman showed that his sense of humour is also on the money while taking author Michael B. Davie on a tour of his residence.*

– PHOTO BY PHILIPPA DAVIE

DeGroote is also the founder and largest financial supporter of the Michael G. DeGroote School of Business at McMaster University. Taking a studied, academic approach, the innovative business school, much like the BAC, is hatching new generations of business leaders.

And, to this short list of impressive entrepreneurial success stories, let's add another famous name: Ron Joyce, co-founder of the Tim Hortons empire. If there's a limit to the market for great-tasting coffee and baked goods, Joyce hasn't found it yet. His familiar Tim Hortons outlets seem to be popping up everywhere. We're finding we have many friends along the way.

Joyce also initiated and engineered the merger with Wendy's. He's now the largest single shareholder of a fast food giant which delights in establishing combo stores, allowing patrons to munch on a Wendy's hamburger, then follow up with Tim Hortons coffee and donuts for dessert.

But I'm getting ahead of myself.

We'll take a far more detailed look at DeGroote, the business school, Joyce, and Howard in the pages ahead. If you've turned to this chapter for truly inspiring success stories, read on.

*Success Stories*

# Michael G. DeGroote

A warm Bermuda breeze gently brushes Mike DeGroote's smiling face as he steers his luxury boat through sun-dappled, bright blue waters.

In his early sixties, but looking years younger, the rugged billionaire businessman is clearly in his element: At the helm, in control, with all of paradise and beyond stretching before his steely gaze.

DeGroote points out a sunken ship, schools of brightly coloured fish and coral reefs as he takes my family and I on a tour of Bermuda's smaller islands.

As I plunk myself down on the first mate's chair beside DeGroote, it occurs to me that the last guest in this chair was former U.S. President Jimmy Carter.

It also occurs to me that DeGroote could have left the driving to one of his staff. Yet it's typical of his hands-on approach, that his own weathered hands keep us moving in the right direction.

At 43 feet in length, the boat is just seven feet shy of being officially classed as a yacht, prompting DeGroote to dub the vessel 'La Petite.'

Our congenial host decides we'll lunch at a resort on the far side of the main island. But as 'La Petite' nears the dock in waters that have now become choppy, he expresses concern that a smaller boat has left his craft little room to dock.

I suggest we go elsewhere. But DeGroote is determined to keep his plans on course. With the precision of a driving school instructor, he deftly parks 'La Petite' as astonished diners look on.

While we dine at a beachside table, DeGroote assists my daughter Sarah in untying a troublesome knot from her running shoe laces. Passers-by, glimpsing this happy, domestic scene, could be excused if they failed to recognize one of the world's most successful businessmen.

And DeGroote's success is indeed the stuff legends are made of.

Forbes magazine's International 500 lists him as one of the world's richest persons. Forbes estimates his fortune at over $1.2 billion US (approaching $2 billion CDN) and ranks him as the fourth-richest Canadian, ahead of Galen Weston and behind Kenneth Thomson (also ranked as fifth-richest person in the world), the Irving family and Charles Bronfman.

Of these five billionaire Canadians, only one, DeGroote, did not inherit his wealth. He earned it. And DeGroote's undiminished ability to amass a vast fortune by his own hands, in a single lifetime, is all the more impressive given the obstacles he faced in his youth.

Born on a farm in West Flanders, Belgium, in 1933, Michael George DeGroote saw his childhood stripped of innocence by the brutality of the Second World War. He was only 14 years old when his family left war-torn Belgium for Canada in 1948, settling on a tobacco farm in Langton, Ontario, about 60 miles south-west of Hamilton.

> "I think it meant that I had to work twice as hard to succeed . . . there really is no substitute for a good education."

"Belgium was in major disarray, due to the Second World War and there was talk that there could be a third war," DeGroote recalls, his gravel voice revealing the barest trace of a Flemish accent. "I couldn't speak much English back then except for 'yes', 'okay' and a few swear words."

Faced with a language barrier and a difficult period of adjustment, DeGroote took advantage of a now-defunct Ontario law allowing youth as young as 14 years of age to drop out of school. He has never attended an Ontario school.

Yet, despite his subsequent success, the hard-driving business tycoon regrets never having extended his formal education beyond the equivalent of Grade 10.

"I think it meant that I had to work twice as hard to succeed . . . there really is no substitute for a good education," says the founder of the Michael G. DeGroote School of Business who contributed $3 million to establish the entrepreneurially spirited school at McMaster University.

DeGroote's own entrepreneurial spirit emerged just a few years after he arrived in Canada. In the early 1950s, an 18-year-old DeGroote bought his first truck – a two-ton army vehicle – and went into business hauling manure from the London area to farms in Langton and Tillsonburg.

By the mid-1950s, DeGroote had expanded his first business to include a second truck and a tractor to work area farms plus four gravel dump trucks to work a Woodstock quarry.

By 1957, he had expanded his fleet to about 30 trucks and formed Langton Contracting Co. Ltd., setting up operations at Elliot Lake, then a booming uranium mining town.

Two years later, DeGroote made a now legendary acquisition when he borrowed $75,000 to buy Laidlaw Transport Ltd., a small Hagersville trucking business from owner Robert Laidlaw.

But DeGroote's emerging business empire was dealt a staggering body blow when an unforeseen plunge in the uranium market prompted an exodus of people and business from Elliot Lake. The population of the northern Ontario town fell to 6,000 people from 28,000. DeGroote's own fortunes fell just as fast.

DeGroote tried to rebuild the business in Sudbury but the financial wounds were too deep. In 1962, Langton Contracting went bankrupt, owing nearly $500,000 to 175 creditors. A year later DeGroote also declared personal bankruptcy with total liabilities exceeding $450,000.

"I kept Laidlaw, but I went from driving Cadillacs and living in a rather nice house to driving a rusty, used car and living in a small rented place," he recalls.

"It taught me a lesson that's stayed with me – you can't overextend yourself financially," adds DeGroote whose subsequent corporate empires have been free of the heavy debt loads that have caused the fall of lesser giants.

Just four months after declaring bankruptcy, DeGroote was discharged, allowing him to get back in business with a clean slate – and no obligation to repay his creditors.

▶
*Typically at the helm in business and recreation, Michael DeGroote steers his boat 'La Petite' across the open waters.*
*– PHOTO BY PHILIPPA DAVIE*

*Success Stories*

# Michael G. DeGroote

## Michael G. DeGroote

*The Atlantic Ocean provides a breath-taking backdrop for the Bermuda setting of Michael DeGroote's palatial estate.*
– PHOTO BY PHILIPPA DAVIE

But DeGroote's *own* moral code went beyond legal limits. Within six years, he'd paid back his creditors.

"I know that legally I didn't have to pay people back but I did because I felt it was the right thing to do," he explains. "These people lent me money in good faith and I felt responsible regardless of what the bankruptcy laws said."

It was the right thing to do – and it earned DeGroote an enduring reputation as a man of his word, someone who doesn't forget the people who have invested and believed in him.

Laidlaw, purchased with borrowed money, was far from an overnight success.

"It was so heavily leveraged that it was six years before I could draw a salary – and it wasn't until I took it public in 1969 that I could get any money out," recalls the former Dundas resident who took 30 years from his 1959 purchase of Laidlaw to build it into a $2 billion-a-year giant.

Canada's Grand Acquisitor had bought some 500 companies on Laidlaw's behalf, transforming Laidlaw in the process.

The company, which moved its headquarters to Hamilton and later Burlington, grew to become the third-largest waste management firm in North America, second-largest hazardous waste company and largest operator of school buses.

In 1988, DeGroote stunned the financial community by selling his Laidlaw shares to Canadian Pacific for $500 million. That same year, Laidlaw had been hailed as the number one growth stock in Canada – for the 17th year in a row.

DeGroote stayed on as Laidlaw's chief executive officer for two more years. And, it continued to grow by leaps and bounds to achieve market capitalization of over $6 billion US (fifth largest in Canada) by the time DeGroote resigned in mid-1990.

DeGroote took a huge tax hit – but it was also his last tax hit. He gathered his fortune together and moved to a new home amid the palm trees and the gentle breezes of Bermuda.

A proud Canadian, DeGroote retains his Canadian citizenship and passport, he remains a director of Calgary-based Gulf Canada Resources and he has been named an Officer of Canada for his sizeable contribution to the country. He also received an Honourary 'Doctor of Law' degree from McMaster University.

The Canadian connections of Michael G. DeGroote, O.C., L.L.D., include $5 million funding for the Michael G. DeGroote Foundation for epilepsy research at McMaster University, funding for recreation facilities at McMaster and Hillfield-Strathallan College and, of course, the Michael G. DeGroote School of Business at McMaster.

DeGroote also spends more than two months of every year in Canada, mainly in Burlington, visiting family, including daughter Joni, son Tim, son Michael Jr., who runs Westbury International, and son Gary, who runs GWD Investments.

*Success Stories*

# Michael G. DeGroote

While still a senior journalist with The Hamilton Spectator, I was fortunate to land an exclusive interview with the Canadian tycoon within weeks of his arrival in Bermuda.

The island is free of income taxes and capital gains taxes. And, DeGroote left no doubt his move was in large part a necessity to avoid ongoing taxation in Canada, at a rate exceeding 50 per cent, which would have severely depleted his income.

He also observed that Bermuda was more conducive to estate planning and it featured convenient air links to the North American markets.

"Canada is a hell of a great country," asserted the one-time owner of the CFL Hamilton Tiger-Cats. "All my original success came from there," he adds. "This was not an easy decision."

DeGroote also made it clear that this was not a retirement move.

My exclusive Spectator stories detailed a new business empire in the making. That empire is being built on the foundations of his holding company Westbury Bermuda – which today controls several companies in North America and Europe – and his ownership stake in Republic Industries.

I caught up with DeGroote again in June 1997 while working on my book, Success Stories.

It was apparent that the Bermuda lifestyle still agreed with my well-tanned host as he spoke of business and life at his palatial seaside home and corporate offices at the capital city of Hamilton.

In March 1991, within three months of moving to Bermuda, he'd bought control of Republic, based in Houston, Texas.

"I'm a deal junkie," DeGroote says, during an interview at his offices.

"The guy who controlled Republic was in financial trouble and wanted me to buy. I didn't really want the company, so I made what I thought was a low-ball offer – and he accepted. I was hooked again."

Within four months of the takeover, DeGroote had completely changed the board – and former president Thomas Fatjo was out the door.

"I had control – but I had inherited a real dog's breakfast of a company," DeGroote recalls. "It took three years to rebuild it into a viable company."

DeGroote then enlisted a brilliant former competitor, Wayne Huizenga, previously chairman of the giant Waste Management Corp., the world's largest waste management firm.

Huizenga was unwilling to invest as long as Republic's troubled hazardous waste division remained part of the company. DeGroote had already spun the company out into two publicly traded entities, Republic Industries Inc. and Republic Environmental Systems Inc., the former hazardous waste division.

With the spinout completed, Huizenga invested in Republic Industries. DeGroote, who had been hands-on managing the company until then, decided to turn operating management of Republic Industries over to Huizenga in May 1995.

At that time, Republic Industries' market capitalization (number of shares issued multiplied by the price per share) rang in at $110 million U.S.

Just two years later, the market capitalization exceeded $10 billion U.S. The incredible gains were pleasing to shareholders, particularly the largest single shareholder, Michael G. DeGroote, who initially held 49 per cent of the shares.

DeGroote also profited handsomely when he invested in a little-known company Huizenga put together from a group of video stores. Both men have done very well with Blockbuster Video.

*A proud Canadian, Michael DeGroote retains his Canadian citizenship and flies the Maple Leaf along with the flags of the U.S. and Bermuda at his estate in Bermuda.*
– PHOTO BY PHILIPPA DAVIE

Success Stories

# Michael G. DeGroote

*With his private jet ready for take-off, Michael DeGroote sets out to explore new business horizons.*
– PHOTO BY PHILIPPA DAVIE

Such triumphs aside, DeGroote still had Republic Environmental and was looking for a solution. It arrived in the form of the Alliance group of insurance companies. The privately held Alliance group wanted to go public and saw a merger with the publicly listed Republic Environmental as the fastest way to achieve a stock market listing.

Alliance began pressing DeGroote to make such a merger happen.

For DeGroote, the pressure was wonderful. His Republic Environmental company was barely worth $12 million (US) on a fully capitalized basis. Shares were languishing around the $2 (US) mark, he explains, "because the company had problems, real and perceived, and nobody was buying its stock."

In contrast, the Alliance group of insurance firms were enjoying annual revenue of $35.7 million (US) – and they wanted to merge with Republic Environmental. DeGroote finally said yes.

To help get the new publicly listed International Alliance company off to a good start, DeGroote invested another $5 million (US) in the company. That investment was matched by Huizenga "and we thought the share price might climb from $2 to $6," recalls DeGroote.

Instead, headlines reporting that both DeGroote and Huizenga were investing millions in the new firm sent share prices soaring to $40 (US) in the span of a few weeks, with demand for the stock grossly exceeding the number of shares issued.

A stock split ensued and shares were selling in mid-1997 for $10 (US) each, or $20 (US) on a pre-split basis.

"The bad news is, the shares dropped to $20 from $40 – the good news is, they started out at $2," chuckles DeGroote, who is also the largest single shareholder of International Alliance, with 49 per cent of the original stock.

And DeGroote continues to play a hands-on role which includes supervising acquisitions, directly handling investing on Wall Street and personally writing company financial reports.

Describing International Alliance as "my pet," DeGroote now intends to "spend several years building it up. It's well-managed, has great shareholder value – I'm excited about its potential."

DeGroote feels the insurance industry and business out-sourcing services are "ripe for consolidation," and he's been making that happen in a big way, shaping and redefining the industry in the process.

Just as DeGroote built Laidlaw into a giant by acquiring hundreds of smaller firms, he's been acquiring a steady stream of small insurance and business out-sourcing firms, integrating them into the larger company while employing economies of scale and service networks to maximize cost-efficiencies and offer customers an array of services at low cost.

International Alliance has gone beyond the bounds of an insurance company. It has diversified into financial planning, accounting, human resource management, payroll services and other out-sourcing services for small to mid-sized firms of five to 100 employees – and all at very competitive prices. This is a largely untapped market as the normal cost of such a package of services would restrict its availability to larger firms.

"We'll let these small firms concentrate on being good entrepreneurs – while we take over all of their paperwork," asserts DeGroote, "and we're looking at a huge market for these services."

As I accompany DeGroote to his private jet, he elaborates on the need to remove obstacles, including paperwork, regulatory and government reports, or lack of education which can stop entrepreneurs from reaching full potential.

"We have to remove the obstacles, the distractions, and give our young entrepreneurs the tools they need to succeed," DeGroote explains on boarding his New York City-bound jet.

"It's important that entrepreneurs focus their energy on chasing their dream."

*Success Stories*

# Michael G. DeGroote

Michael G. DeGroote offers the following tips for success:

➤ Clearly define your goals and foster a strong desire to succeed. Focus on goals and priorities.

➤ Start or acquire a business which suits your abilities, one which you will genuinely enjoy devoting a lot of time to. Then, devote the necessary time to make the firm prosper and grow.

➤ Use determination, a methodology and consistency of approach to carry out goals. Expect to work long and hard to achieve these goals and to sacrifice much of your "personal" time.

➤ Make sure you link up with the right people whose skill sets complement your own. Be certain everyone has a clear understanding of the company's direction and your own expectations.

➤ Realize your employees generate the profit. You and the rest of the management group are simply overhead.

➤ Keep your managers and layers of management to a minimum to improve communications.

➤ Do the most with the least.

➤ Focus on creating shareholder value.

➤ Do not over extend yourself. Too many entrepreneurs take on too much debt far too early and find they cannot handle the carrying costs.

➤ Keep your overhead low, and your operations lean and mean.

➤ Make commitments and keep them. Be as good as your word.

➤ Initially, grow the company slowly without resorting to excessive financing. "Banks always lend in good faith and they can sometimes be talked into lending too much – and then they get blamed for a business failure," says DeGroote.

"You have to limit your borrowing to match your ability to pay."

*Billionaire Michael G. DeGroote continues to make the right calls in business.*
*– PHOTO BY PHILIPPA DAVIE*

➤ Focus on creating high quality services or products, meeting customer needs and desires.

➤ Avoid running up large debts.

It was six to seven years before Michael DeGroote was able to draw a meaningful salary from Laidlaw because he had leveraged heavily and his total debt servicing costs were huge.

As DeGroote points out: "You have to walk a long time before you can run. Success doesn't happen overnight."

"Grow your business step by step, slowly, and as you get comfortable with the pace, you can start sprinting, faster and faster," DeGroote advises.

"The first million is the hardest," he says. "But there are more millionaires and billionaires now than ever before."

➤ Be willing to take on risk. But try to ensure this is manageable risk that is necessary to undertake in order for you to capitalize on the business opportunities that exist today.

➤ Foster teamwork and put in place the best team you can assemble.

➤ Listen carefully to employees, assist them where possible and always reward them for achievements.

➤ Never lock yourself into anything. Be prepared to change.

➤ Do not brood over your mistakes. Focus on solutions. Make your worklife enjoyable and satisfying.

➤ Take a hard look in the mirror and raise your own expectations of yourself. Says DeGroote: "When you're through improving, you're through."

*Success Stories*

# Michael G. DeGroote School Of Business

It's an incubator hatching the next generation of entrepreneurs.

And the Michael G. DeGroote School of Business at McMaster University is ensuring that tomorrow's leaders receive an enviable business education with an entrepreneurial edge.

The school, named in honour of its chief benefactor, billionaire businessman Mike DeGroote, is endeavouring to instill its programs with a degree of DeGroote's risk-taking business savvy.

"The emphasis on entrepreneurialism hasn't come about to the degree we'd like – and certainly not to the degree Michael DeGroote would want," notes David Conrath, Dean of the business school.

"But our curriculum is evolving, moving in that direction," Conrath says in an interview at his campus office.

"We're getting business professors to think along that line," he explains, "even though they may have been trained in big business and lack an entrepreneurial background. Few business schools are doing this. It's not an easy thing to teach."

"We can certainly provide courses, information and advice," he adds.

"But entrepreneurialism is as much a state of mind and experience as it is a state of education – yet we can cater to entrepreneurialism and improve our ability to relate to small companies. After all, many of our grads go to work for small companies – or start up their own firms."

"We held a day-long workshop on entrepreneurs – which featured Michael DeGroote as a speaker – and we hope to make this an annual event," offers Conrath whose business school motto is: Hit Your Career Path Running. "However, the school itself is more entrepreneurial than its curriculum," he cautions.

Examples of the DeGroote school's entrepreneurial approach include an off-campus MBA program, currently available at Cambridge Memorial Hospital. It will also be introduced in 1998 to Quantum, a rising software house.

Clients are charged a fixed rate fee to have staff take MBA courses at work. Courses are also somewhat tailored to meet the needs of employers. "We're the first business school in Canada to take the MBA program and place it right on the client's premises," Conrath says proudly.

In 1997, the school introduced, at Hamilton & District Chamber of Commerce offices, its MVP (Most Valuable Performer) upgrading program aimed at improving decision-making by middle and upper management levels, while turning a profit for the school itself. Coming soon: a stock market trading room to foster investment knowledge.

The school is also establishing several niche areas of expertise, making it the

> " *It taught us how to learn, how to think in business terms, how to ask the right questions – and those are all valuable skills.* "

business school to turn to for curriculum on the management of innovation and new technology, health services management and financial services management.

McMaster, ranked by Maclean's and other magazines as one of Canada's most innovative and research-intensive universities, has also made innovation a focal point of its business school.

The MINT (Management of Innovation & New Technology) Research Centre at the school places an emphasis on practical research, says MINT director Chris Bart.

Bart says the need to research effective ways of managing innovation and technology was recognized with MINT's 1992 founding. Only five of 55 faculty were then focused in this area.

That number doubled by 1994 when MINT designed and launched Canada's first MBA stream on the management of innovation. The same year, MINT also launched the world's first international e-mail network – boasting more than 1,000 members – on the management of innovation.

MINT, a free-standing, privately funded entity, now has a critical mass of people involved in conducting research.

DeGroote has helped with $500,000 in funding and another $250,000 has been secured from other major corporate sponsors, including the Royal Bank, Nortel, DuPont Canada, and the Society of Management Accountants of Ontario.

"Our main goal is to do research that matters into the management of innovation and new technology," says Bart, "and we want to be Canada's pre-eminent research centre."

By mid-1997, MINT had created an environment for collaborative and interdisciplinary research in the field of innovation management.

MINT has also produced more than 60 research papers, held a conference on innovative entrepreneurs and initiated 24 projects. Bart enthusiastically hails the research centre as a success, in part because "very few people ever drop out."

The school as a whole is similarly successful. Conrath notes virtually 100 per cent of the MBAs achieve job placement on graduation and about 85 per cent of undergraduate Commerce grads find work, "with the primary reason being our excellent co-op and internship programs."

Bob Hodgson, public affairs director for the business school, says employers often comment that "our grads roll up their sleeves and get right to work."

Of course, these future business leaders include entrepreneurs, who go on to create their own jobs and opportunities.

Brothers Phil and Rich Smart are relatively recent business school grads who founded Visual Applications Software Inc. in Burlington in the early 1990s.

Their software, which organizes a company's customer calls and contracts, helped them grow to 25 employees and $4 million in annual revenue before they sold the company, in January 1997, to Columbus, Ohio-based Symix Software Inc., for an undisclosed sum.

Of their education at the business school, Phil Smart asserts: "It taught us how to learn, how to think in business terms, how to ask the right questions – and those are all valuable skills."

▶
*Tomorrow's entrepreneurs are in a class of their own at the Michael G. DeGroote School of Business. The school makes its home at McMaster University.*
– PHOTO BY DAVID GRUGGEN

# Michael G. DeGroote School Of Business

Success 69 Stories

# Ron Joyce

Canada's enduring fast food love affair has an ardent suitor in Ron Joyce. The co-founder of Tim Hortons restaurants, is successfully courting a seemingly insatiable public appetite for great coffee, soups and baked goods.

He's also developing a 1,000-acre resort in Nova Scotia with marina and 5,000-foot runway to accommodate fly-in vacationers eager to fish, hunt or golf on a professionally designed golf course. He now resides in Calgary and he's also part-owner of the NHL Calgary Flames.

And as International Wendy's largest single shareholder, he's soaring to new entrepreneurial heights to serve our yen for tasty hamburgers, french fries, salads and stuffed pita sandwiches.

I found Joyce in good spirits and cradling a cup of Tim Hortons coffee as he emerged from his private jet at Jetport, his new multi-million-dollar, 40,000-square-foot facility at Hamilton Airport. In business to meet the travel needs of executives, the Jetport facility also has a seaplane and Lear jet.

"My focus is still on Tim Hortons," Joyce smiles reassuringly when asked of his diversified interests. "And there's still plenty of room for growth, particularly with Tim Hortons-and-Wendy's combo restaurants," adds the former Hamiltonian, stepping onto the tarmac. By mid-1997, there were already 65 combo restaurants with another 50 in development.

Joyce – who initiated and drove both the combo concept and the 1995 merger with Wendy's – is pleased his high quality Hortons chain has aligned with another high quality entity: Ohio-based Wendy's, the world's third-largest fast-food chain with some 5,000 restaurants.

Tim Hortons is Canada's largest coffee and donuts chain with 48 per cent of the market. "We serve more customers in this country than anybody else," Joyce says.

There are currently 1,500 stores and that number should grow to 2,000 by the year 2000, according to Joyce, the Senior Chairman of TDL (Tim Donut Limited) Group, the Oakville-based licensing company for Tim Hortons franchises.

In 1996, Wendy's system-wide sales revenue surpassed $7.5 billion. Of this sum, Tim Hortons – a part of Wendy's since the 1995 merger – accounted for $905 million, up from $835 million in 1995. Over $1 billion in revenue is expected by the year 2000.

The impressive revenue numbers seem a world away from Joyce's modest origins as a boy in Tatamagouche, Nova Scotia.

In 1947, at the age of 16, Joyce left the struggling Maritimes in search of job opportunities in Ontario.

After moving to Hamilton to work in a factory, he left Firestone in 1951 to join the Royal Canadian Navy and serve in the Korean Conflict.

> "Right from the start, our focus and our efforts were dedicated to becoming a successful franchise company."

Joyce would also serve in the Navy Reserves for eight years. He returned to Hamilton in 1956 and began nine years with the Hamilton Police force.

In 1963, his entrepreneurial spirit led him to buy a Dairy Queen franchise.

When he was unable to get a second DQ location, Joyce instead took over the first-ever Tim Hortons store in 1965. At the time it was the only store owned by Horton, the legendary NHL Toronto Maple Leafs defenceman, who founded the Ottawa Street, Hamilton store in 1964.

"Tim and I developed quite a friendship," says Joyce, recalling his acquisition of the then-struggling store.

By 1967, Joyce had opened two more shops and he and Horton became full partners. Joyce grew the business while Horton pursued a 25-year hockey career, mainly with the Leafs but later with the Rangers, Penguins and Sabres.

"Right from the start, our focus and our efforts were dedicated to becoming a successful franchise company," Joyce recollects. "We knew this was the best and fastest way to grow."

Also from the beginning, Joyce placed an emphasis on the company owning or lease-holding the physical locations the franchisees located in.

"We wanted to own as much of the real estate as possible – to control our own destiny," recalls Joyce who got his pilot's license after Tim Hortons expanded to Cornwall. He bought a Cherokee 235 single-engine plane to more easily conduct real estate deals as the business grew.

Tim Horton died in a car accident in 1974. Following his death, Joyce bought his shares and took over as sole owner of the chain which then numbered 40 stores.

In Horton's honour, Joyce established the Tim Horton Children's Foundation, a non-profit, charitable organization which runs summer camps, for under-privileged children, located at Tatamagouche, Nova Scotia; Parry Sound, Ontario; Kananaskis County, Alberta; and Quvon, Quebec, with another to open soon in the U.S.

Tireless charitable work as chairman of the foundation earned Joyce the 1991 Gary Wright Humanitarian Award – and a 1992 appointment to the Order of Canada.

He has also been named a Fellow of the Hostelry Institute and has earned the Ontario Hostelry Institute Gold Award as Chain Restaurant Operator of 1992.

Joyce has also received an Honourary Doctorate of Commerce from St. Mary's University at Halifax and the McGill University Management Achievement Award. And he's only the second recipient of the Canadian Franchise Association's Lifetime Achievement Award.

It's a full life of accomplishment. But Joyce shows no signs of slowing down. He speaks enthusiastically of his future plans to take the Hortons empire into Europe, South America and Asia.

And he continues to take pride in Tim Hortons' Hamilton roots.

Although the Hamilton area has one of the highest concentrations of coffee and donut stores anywhere, Joyce knows there is still room for more locations either at stand-alone sites or at kiosks in gas bars, hospitals or retail stores.

The demand is clearly there. Take it from Joyce: You've always got time for Tim Hortons.

▶
*With Tim Hortons coffee in hand, Ron Joyce emerges from his corporate jet.*
– PHOTO BY DAVID GRUGGEN

# Ron Joyce

Success Stories

# John Howard

John Howard savours the character of fine wines.

But success for this renowned vintner flows from his own character – and his ability to bring out the best in others.

In the exacting arts of winemaking and human relations, the owner-proprietor of Vineland Estates Winery has proven a sound judge of character. "This is as much a people business as it is a wine business," Howard, 46, explains over a crisp glass of Vineland Estates Riesling Reserve.

"And when dealing with people, I tend to follow my gut feeling," he adds, raising his glass at the winery's patio restaurant.

Clearly more at ease living his business philosophy than discussing it, Howard pauses for a moment to take in the idyllic setting overlooking vineyards, woodlands and Lake Ontario. To the east rises the mist of Niagara Falls. To the north lies a ghostly image of Toronto's skyline.

"What's in your heart and your head should come out of your mouth," rejoins Howard. "And never, ever put yourself in a position where you feel you have to cross the street rather than meet up with someone you did business with in the past," he adds. "You should always feel comfortable with your approach to business and people."

With this, Howard excuses himself to quietly greet and chat with patrons. His pleasant approach ensures their visit is enjoyable, memorable. "You're from Quebec?" he queries a group of diners. "How was your journey?"

Howard's own life journey is a stretching grapevine, twisting towards a satisfying fruition. Vineland Estates' congenial host began worklife in the 1970s looking down on society. Literally.

He was a high steelworker working hundreds of feet in the air on office towers under construction. The work gave him an enlarged neck, a firm grip and a taste for panoramic views. The work also helped finance a liberal arts education. The young roughneck became immersed in the arts, studying and appreciating humanity's finest expressions and achievements.

After serving as a Xerox salesman, he co-founded the Canon dealership Office Equipment Hamilton.

"One of the lessons I learned, is that people don't buy technology, they buy people." Howard recalls. "They buy track records and a perceived level of expertise in an area of discipline."

He also found that "people solve problems – not technology, which is only a tool. Take away the human element and all you've got is a hulk plugged in a wall with a start button."

Howard earned success by developing long-term customer relationships. "I view business as more of a relationship than a contractual matter," he says.

He became a millionaire by merging with OE Canada; a multi-millionaire in 1992 after Canon North America bought OE Canada. At age 38 he paid $1 million in taxes every two years.

> *I realized making money isn't satisfying on its own ... I won't do business unless it involves people I like and respect.*

"I benefitted from an accelerated economy in the 1980s, but how much do you need," he says. "I realized making money isn't satisfying on its own. I reached a point where I won't do business unless it involves people I like and respect. I found those people at Vineland Estates."

It was then that Howard cancelled plans to take a year off and instead purchased Vineland Estates, the picturesque 78-acre vineyard and winery not far from his palatial home, a 14-room retreat, dubbed Castle Howard, complete with turrets and resembling a French chateau.

He downplays his role while paying homage to winery founder Hermann Weis, a 16th generation vintner from Germany's Mosel Valley. Howard even erected a plaque honouring the founder's pioneering work in transplanting vinifera plants and in advancing Niagara winemaking.

"I'm just a steward who has the responsibility of continuing high standards set by the Weis family who created all this," insists Howard, who went on to invest millions of dollars in restoring a carriage house on the property, originally a mixed farm dating from the 1840s. Kitchen facilities are staffed by skilled chefs. He's invested heavily in winemaking facilities and grape production.

Howard can take pride in the contribution of lasting value he's made to Vineland Estates. It's something fans of this winery have come to appreciate – as they savour crisp wines and great food in a setting of unrivalled beauty. It's a relaxing, almost magical escape from the everyday.

Then there's his investment in people. In an age when many employers are reducing employee benefits, he has taken a refreshingly paternalistic approach, bestowing scholarships on staff members who exemplify a strong work ethic and great customer service. Not surprisingly, the service is consistently superb.

While relying on skilled staff to continue producing excellent wines, Howard has proven highly adept at charting a successful strategic plan for Vineland Estates.

And it's a plan which places a strong emphasis on export sales: By 1996, Vineland Estates was producing 20,000 cases (240,000 bottles) of Rieslings and other fine wines annually from its own vineyards. About 80 per cent is exported to U.S., England and Pacific Rim markets or sold on-site. The rest is sold through conventional distribution in Ontario.

"Niagara wines have achieved international standards and are winning numerous awards for quality," explains Howard, "and I've never seen any reason to be reticent about exporting our excellent products to world markets."

With retail sales up dramatically, a doubling of restaurant sales and the overall success of Vineland Estates, Howard is now involved with his Niagara Land Company partners – Weis, Dieter Jahnke and Paul Mazza – in developing other lands into vineyards and wineries.

Much has been achieved by Howard. But there are new horizons to conquer, new culinary concepts to introduce, new facilities to build, new vinifera to plant – and new award-winning wines to produce.

▶

*John Howard and daughter Erin share a quiet moment at Vineland Estates patio restaurant. Howard's castle-like home is pictured at the beginning of this chapter.*
– PHOTO BY DAVID GRUGGEN

*Success Stories*

# John Howard

Success 73 Stories

CKOC/1150
eating circuit cafe
OPEN TO THE PUBLIC
The Hamilton Spectator

# CHAPTER 6

# Media Managers

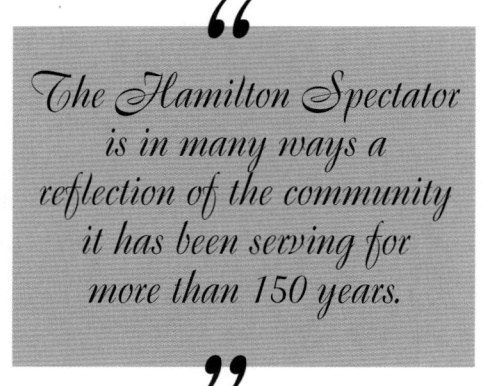

# Media Managers

In today's Information Age, getting fast, accurate and detailed reports, data and images has become an accepted necessity. Information is a valuable commodity. Those with vital information prosper and grow. Those without are better left to a book which is not entitled Success Stories.

In our sprawling economic region, no look at information suppliers would be complete without an examination of the largest daily newspaper between Niagara Falls and Oakville.

The Hamilton Spectator is in many ways a reflection of the community it serves, distilling information and opinion in tune with local values and interests.

Of course, the venerable daily newspaper is also a business, subject to the same economic highs and lows which have led companies everywhere to downsize, restructure and reassess their approach. Having been part of the Hamilton community for more than 150 years, The Spectator has joined other businesses in weathering every change in the local economy.

In the mid-1990s, The Spectator began recovering from the 1990s recession by restructuring and changing its approach to one offering more direct appeal to the community it serves. The Spectator is now read by 60 per cent of the adult population in the newspaper's primary market area of Hamilton-Wentworth, Burlington and Grimsby, according to NADbank '97, the annual newspapers market study of 27 urban centres across Canada. That's a total of nearly 300,000 readers Monday through Friday while Saturday's paper averages some 320,000 readers.

Add in occasional readers who buy only a few issues of the paper each week, and total Spectator readership exceeds 77 per cent of area adults, nearly 390,000 people.

In contrast, The Toronto Sun is read by 18 per cent of Hamilton area adults, The Toronto Star by 13 per cent and The Globe and Mail by 10 per cent, according to NADbank '97.

Like many other newspapers across Canada, The Spectator's circulation had been in decline for a number of years, particularly through much of the 1990s. However, by the summer of 1997, circulation had stabilized and then started to grow.

In the spring of 1997, The Spec's paid circulation, – once at a peak level of 150,000 copies – stood at approximately 103,000 copies on weekdays and about 130,000 copies on Saturdays, according to an ABC (Audit Bureau of Circulation) report.

By the fall of 1997, circulation had climbed to 108,000 and Publisher Pat Collins was expressing confidence a level of 110,000 copies would be reached by year's end.

Collins cites The Spec's determination to put out a better paper as a leading factor behind the circulation gains. Indeed, surveys on readership interests consistently rank local news as the number one area of interest, followed by national and international news.

The Spectator has responded to reader desires with in-depth news and commentary sections, including Observer on Saturdays, World View Weekly on Fridays and Home Fires, a regular foreign news feature, appealing to Hamilton's foreign-born population (Hamilton trails only Toronto and Vancouver for having the highest percentage of its population born outside of Canada).

In 1997, The Spectator also improved its business coverage with weekly Enterprise and Computer sections. A weekday Life section has been added and the newspaper has invested over $2.4 million to upgrade its press equipment, reducing waste and improving quality in the process.

The Spectator's parent company, Southam Inc., also owns the local Brabant chain of community newspapers, publishing such weeklies as Hamilton Mountain News, Dundas Star-Journal, Ancaster News, Stoney Creek News, Flamborough News, Pelham Herald, and the Real Estate News and Buyers' Guide.

After a year as Editor of The Phoenix, Mohawk College's student newspaper in the mid-1970s, I spent a couple of years as regional news editor, columnist, reporter, occasional editorial writer and sometime photographer for the Brabant weeklies, a chain where few reporters were confined to that role alone.

Then, as now, the chain's success is tied to its unwavering dedication to providing community news. While The Spectator is a reflection of the wider community, the weeklies reflect the concerns and interests of the smaller suburban centres, sometimes at the neighbourhood and local school level.

Delivered free of charge to a mass audience, the weeklies, with their lower advertising rates, serve a niche market with a mix of small-town news and views.

There are also a number of specialty publications in the area, including Hamilton magazine and Biz magazine. And, there's The Business Executive, an Oakville-based business monthly, published and operated by the husband-and-wife team of Tom and Wendy Peters.

The Niagara region is dominated by The St. Catharines Standard, a mid-sized daily newspaper with a solid reputation for journalistic excellence. This region also boasts the dailies Niagara Falls Review and The Welland Tribune, another of my former haunts. As a Tribune reporter and columnist in the late 1970s, I covered everything from courts and crime to City Hall, Niagara Regional Government, and politics at every level.

Serving Niagara, Hamilton, even Toronto, is ONtv, the former CHCH-TV, which exemplifies, in a broadcast sense, Hamilton's role as the hub of wider economic region.

This region also has one of the nation's liveliest radio markets, characterized by 820 CHAM country music radio, Hometown Radio 900 CHML and Oldies 1150 CKOC.

CKOC, Ontario's oldest radio station and second only to Montreal's CFCF as Canada's oldest station, celebrated its 75th anniversary in 1997.

Founded in 1922 by Herb Slack, CKOC inadvertently gave rise to a rival radio station in 1926, legend has it, when Slack pulled the plug on a First United Church broadcast which ventured into politics with a lecture on prohibition. The incensed parishioners formed Maple Leaf Broadcasting and started up CHML.

> "The Hamilton Spectator is in many ways a reflection of the community it has been serving for more than 150 years."

Success Stories

# Media Managers

▲
*Expansion into new markets has created new challenges and new opportunities for ONtv – formerly Hamilton's CHCH-TV. With a sharper focus and state-of-the-art equipment, including the Delta 1 mobile unit, the television station is sending a clear signal to station viewers that ONtv is committed to excellence in its new broadcasting role. The digital mobile unit, shown above, is contained inside a 53-foot, 35,000-pound trailer.*
*– PHOTO BY DAVID GRUGGEN*

In more recent years, CKOC has adopted an Oldies format, specializing in 1950s-1960s music selected by on-air personality Bob Sherwin. And, CKOC's sister station 102.9 K-Lite FM has the number-one ranked Sunni & Hayes radio show, featuring the dynamic duo of Sunni Genesco and Matt Hayes, who doubles as ONtv's light-hearted weatherman.

CHML proudly bills itself as Hamilton's Hometown Radio, building success from its close association with the community it serves. As we'll see, CHML has positioned itself as an integral part of the Steel City's popular culture and unpretentious identity.

Although part of the advertising, not reporting, sect, Stirling Print-All is another established member of the media positioning itself to capture a larger market share. Stirling is undergoing some gutsy and far-sighted changes with an eye on future growth.

And we've all seen the photographic talents of David Gruggen gracing everything from newspapers, brochures and magazines to exhibits and books – including the one you're holding right now.

We'll take a closer look at David Gruggen, The Spec, ONtv, CHML and Stirling Print-All in a collection of profiles, next.

*Success* 77 *Stories*

# The Hamilton Spectator

The Hamilton Spectator is emphasizing content in a reader-friendly effort to recapture past subscribers – and reach out to a new generation.

"My sense is that a lot of newspapers are in trouble because they felt they should emulate television or appeal to browsers," observes Kirk LaPointe, Spectator Editor in Chief.

"Some newspapers have found circulation in decline as they almost defied the intelligent reader to find anything worth reading," adds LaPointe, who joined The Spectator in January 1997.

"Our job is to appeal to readers," he asserts. "We go big on stories we feel are big. We want our readers to feel we give them the full story on important issues."

LaPointe offers examples of extensive treatment, including Spectator coverage of the Plastimet fire, Hamilton's poor air quality, the extent of area child abuse, and downtown renewal.

"People go through three phases when dealing with a major issue," he says.

"There's a phase of awareness-raising, a coming to terms and finally a resolution phase. Many papers try to compress three phases into two by covering the event and closing it off with a follow-up story."

But the reader is still discussing the issue and needs more information, he says.

"We have to campaign on issues, apportion the space to sustain coverage over a longer period of time. We want to allow the community more time to assess issues on a sustained basis."

LaPointe is making sustained coverage occur through the paper's daily initiative reporting projects.

He's also running more primer boxes that explain the basics of ongoing issues so readers don't lose track of origins and reasons behind anything from geopolitical conflict to local affairs. The boxes act as teaching aids, sharing background information or defining terms and concepts.

"Context is extremely important, yet it's often not included or is cut out of a story," LaPointe adds. "We're conditioning our reporters to make context a key point of the story. I think if we can do that, we'll add value and we'll have one of the best-read papers in the country."

Clarity is also vital, adds the veteran newsman with over 20 years experience, including 17 years with news wire service Canadian Press, the rest with CBC Newsworld and Southam News.

"For example, it's not enough to run a story about the TSE index breaking a barrier – we have to clearly explain what the index is, what it means, why this is important," LaPointe asserts.

"To the credit of the people who work here, we're using a direct form of writing, closer to the way people speak. We're avoiding backing into stories or making the lead paragraph a riddle. We don't assume readers are already well-informed on issues. We're explaining the news."

> "We go big on stories we feel are big. We want our readers to feel we give them the full story on important issues."

Spectator Publisher Pat Collins is also committed to improving content as the surest way of regenerating newspaper advertising and capturing more readers.

Noting the paper is "more active and more supportive of local events," Collins advocates increased coverage of health, education, environment and government issues, along with a "focus on delivering value to our readers and our advertisers."

This 'if-you-build-it-they-will-come' approach seems to be working. After years of decline, advertising is up and The Spec is also attracting readers with a content-rich paper now boasting an average of 44 to 50 pages on weekdays, with much fatter papers on Saturdays.

It's certainly come a long way from the four-page, penny-a-copy Hamilton Spectator and Journal of Commerce that Robert Smiley founded in 1846 with a $150 second-hand printing press.

After Smiley died in 1855, a succession of owners followed until William Southam and William Carey paid $10,000 for the paper in 1877. It was carried on by generations of Southams, becoming the flagship of the nation's largest-circulation newspaper group. The paper continues to be owned by Southam Inc. to this day.

In 1897, The Spectator Printing Co. set up shop in a six-storey James Street building. A 'skyscraper' in its day, it was a converging site for hundreds of newsboys clambering for papers to deliver.

After 28 years, The Spectator moved to a larger site opposite the Royal Connaught Hotel on King Street East in 1921 where it would stay for the next 55 years.

In 1976, The Spectator moved to its present Frid Street building, housing several hundred staff and three presses collectively worth $7.5 million and capable of producing up to 70,000 papers per hour. The Spectator newsroom installed computers in 1981 and upgraded in 1994.

But The Spectator's most impressive changes of late have been improvements to the newspaper itself.

Shortly after LaPointe's arrival, the paper introduced its expansive Enterprise business section. And, former Chatelaine Editor Mildred Istona is helping improve the paper as its new Associate Editor.

There's also a revamped magazine-style Weekend package and the colour comics section now includes children's television listings, sports and news items.

The Sports section features its own weekly editorial page, carrying the opinions of area sports fans. LaPointe hopes to introduce this concept to Business pages in the near future. In addition to local news and views, The Spectator has added Home Fires international stories and such national columnists as Mordecai Richler, Andrew Coyne and Giles Gherson.

But as the paper fattens up with a wealth of analytical pieces, provocative opinion columns, local 'Vignettes' and lengthy investigative reports, it's placing new demands on readers.

"One reader complained it takes too long to read the paper," says LaPointe, shaking his head. "He used to go through the paper in 30 minutes. But today he has trouble finding the two hours it now takes him to read everything of interest. For him, it seems to be a real problem."

If so, it's a problem many Canadian newspapers would love to have.

▶

*Spectator Editor in Chief Kirk LaPointe began pressing for improvements after coming to the paper in January 1997.*
  – PHOTO BY DAVID GRUGGEN

*The Hamilton Spectator*

*Success* 79 *Stories*

# Hometown Radio CHML

Emphasizing its Steel City identity, CHML is positioning itself to retain its current audience and capture the hearts and minds of new generations of Hamilton-area residents.

Proudly billing itself as Hamilton's Hometown Radio, CHML celebrated its 70th anniversary in 1997, making it one of the oldest radio stations in Canada.

At the core of Radio 900 CHML's approach is its dyed-in-the-wool Hamilton identity. This seasoned radio station is as Hamiltonian as you can get. The Steel City is front and centre in the station's focus and approach to everything, from news and views to talk show formats.

And, when the hometown celebrated its 150th anniversary in 1996, it was fitting that Hometown Radio CHML was designated the 'Official Voice' of the city's Sesquicentennial celebrations.

As always, the station was able to draw on a wealth of legendary on-air talent, including newscaster Bill Sturrup.

A 35-year CHML veteran, Sturrup has covered everything for the station from the CANUSA Games to the Ford World Curling Championships.

Sturrup, immortalized with a Media Legend Award at a Grey Cup Legends event, covered the 1996 Grey Cup at Hamilton's Ivor Wynne Stadium where play-by-play coverage was provided by veteran newscaster Bob Hooper.

CHML's strong focus on Hamilton is a sincere tribute to the Ambitious City.

"We're very proud to be a part of this great city," asserts CHML Program Director Darryl Hartwick, noting that CHML's radio roots run deep in Hamilton.

In fact, civic pride has been a CHML hallmark since its inception.

With the station's call letters standing for Canada, Hamilton and Maple Leaf, CHML was founded in 1927 by George Lees with just 50 watts of power.

After a decade of struggle, the late broadcasting legend Ken Soble became station manager and revamped the station to put an emphasis on news and views.

In 1944, Soble bought the radio station and increased its wattage.

The early 1990s witnessed the introduction of a new FM rock station, CJXY FM – better known as Classic Rock Y95. This station followed CHML FM, which was founded in 1964. Three years later, the station was renamed CKDS FM (in honor of Ken D. Soble) and stayed with those call letters until the move to Y95.

In 1997, as CHML celebrated 70 years of broadcasting, the station was using more than 100,000 watts.

Radio buffs can only look back with nostalgia to another era, decades ago, when entire families would pull up chairs to their radio (as physically large as a still-to-be-invented TV set) and listen to news, big bands and drama shows.

> *Radio still plays a central, immediate role in our lives... It can still touch the lives of people everywhere.*

Yet, in many ways, radio still plays a central, immediate role in our lives.

"Radio can still touch the lives of people everywhere," asserts Hooper.

"When a snowstorm happens, people instantly go to the radio to find out what's been cancelled or how much more snow to expect or how bad the roads are and what streets to avoid," he says.

"Radio will never return to its glory days – I don't think those days will ever return," adds the 35-year CHML stalwart.

"Radio has been through some rough times. But radio will always be there."

CHML President and General Manager Don Luzzi says "the hometown personality, news, talk, sports format with continuing commitment to the community, remains a viable and winning combination."

Indeed, CHML on-air personalities are increasingly emphasizing the station's Hamilton-first approach.

For example, Roy Green's Talkline, is again being broadcast from Hamilton after being previously broadcasted simultaneously to Talk 640 via a Toronto studio.

"Hamiltonians are the backbone and the nucleus of the Talkline audience," says Green, the host of Talkline which is one of CHML's most popular programs.

And there's the spirited Hometown Morning Show hosted by 20-year CHML veteran John Hardy, along with the rest of the morning team: Dorie Cowling, Bob Hooper, Casey McKeown and Al Craig.

Hardy's popular oldies music show – Moldy, Goldy and Hardy – entered its 17th year in 1997.

"Dorie, Bob, Casey, Al and I enjoy each other's company," says Hardy. "When we're having a good time, it shows."

CHML's hometown programming continues throughout the day with Lisa Brandt hosting the Midday Talk Show, following by Dr. Laura and new afternoon drive host Dave Spragge whose interactive show invites community input.

Such depth of talent – there are others too numerous to mention – help keep CHML and affiliate FM station Y95 fresh, alive and relevant to listeners.

CHML is the voice of the CFL Hamilton Tiger-Cats, AHL Hamilton Bull Dogs, NHL Toronto Maple Leafs, the Toronto Blue Jays and amateur sports.

Some would argue that CHML is the voice of Hamilton itself.

Finally, there's the radio station's commitment to championing worthy local causes, always keeping the best interests of the Hamilton community at heart.

For example, 1997 marked the 21st year for CHML's Christmas Tree of Hope campaign which, since its inception, has supported various charitable organizations in Hamilton and Burlington.

The idea was the brainchild of Luzzi, who observes that "it's really symbolic of what our station represents."

"Putting something back into the community has been an integral part of CHML ever since it signed on 70 years ago," Luzzi explains.

"Since 1976, everyone on staff has contributed their time and energy to make this campaign a success, enabling us to touch thousands of lives in our hometown community," he adds.

It's this enduring commitment to the Hamilton community, Luzzi says, which has helped make 900 CHML, Hometown Radio "70 Years Strong."

▶

*Happy on the homefront: Veteran CHML employees, left to right, Phil Hitchcock, Barb Fordham, Bill Osborne, Lynn Latimer, Bob Hooper, Ted Townsend.*
– PHOTO BY DAVID GRUGGEN

# Hometown Radio CHML

*Success* 81 *Stories*

# ONtv

As the hub of an important market, Hamilton will always be on TV.

And, this importance ensures ONtv will always be in Hamilton.

Key to continued health and longevity for the former CHCH is its acquisition in 1993 by WIC (Western International Communications Ltd.).

CHCH – Canada's first and largest independent TV station – was fighting a losing battle against much larger networks for market share when the WIC takeover provided a welcome infusion of capital and an alliance with a vastly bigger entity.

An integrated broadcast, communications and entertainment company, WIC encompasses WIC Television Ltd. which also owns stations in Victoria, Vancouver, Kelowna, Lethbridge, Red Deer, Calgary, Edmonton and Montreal, following CRTC approval of WIC's transfer of ownership application to purchase CFCF.

In 1997, WIC established a number of rebroadcast transmitters allowing the Hamilton-based TV station to broadcast its signal to Ottawa and London plus the northern Ontario market via transmitters in Muskoka, North Bay, Sudbury, Sault Ste. Marie and Timmins.

With its expansion into new markets, the former CHCH changed its name to ONtv to reflect its expanded role as an Ontario TV network now reaching 90 per cent of the provincial population.

Indeed, while Hamilton area residents proudly call ONtv their own, the station's signal is actually broadcast across Ontario and into rural and remote communities across the country, including the high Arctic – via the Cancom satellite service.

ONtv now has a reach of more than 4.2 million viewers, coast to coast to coast.

And, this expanded broadcast role – especially across Ontario – is absolutely essential if ONtv is to survive and thrive, asserts Jim Macdonald, president and CEO of WIC Television Ltd., ONtv and WIC Entertainment.

"We compete in arguably the most competitive market in North America where take-overs, mergers and ownership transfers have dramatically changed the landscape of the market," he says.

"But ONtv's future as an Ontario regional television network is secured," Macdonald adds, "and the benefit to WIC is that it gains a strong presence in the important Ontario market."

"We've proven we can compete with Global on an even footing. Some of the programs we've acquired – such as Veronica's Closet and Suddenly Susan – are programs Global wanted. We have the added buying clout that comes with a network. The single biggest issue is programming costs so you have to be big to compete. And we can expose our advertisers to a wider market."

Despite its broader reach, ONtv isn't forgetting its hometown.

"First and foremost," Macdonald asserts, "our commitment is to serve the people of Hamilton and Niagara and our focus will continue here."

> "First and foremost, our commitment is to serve the people of Hamilton and Niagara and our focus will continue here."

ONtv has forged a highly competitive presence in this market, notes Macdonald.

"We're rebuilding and positioning ourselves in a very customer-focused way. Our cornerstones are firmly in place now and they will enable us to move forward with clear objectives and a clear mission."

With programming the cornerstone to a stronger presence, ONtv is focusing its news on the Hamilton-Halton-Niagara area, shoring up its regional base.

Overseeing day-to-day operations at ONtv is Bryan Ellis, the recently named executive vice-president and general manager. Ellis, a television veteran, replaces former executive vice-president Reg McGuire, who retired after 37 years of service at the TV station.

It's been an inspiring evolution for Hamilton's TV station.

Founded by Ken Soble in 1954, "Lucky Channel 11" began broadcasting as a privately owned affiliate of the CBC Network. In 1961, under Soble's leadership, CHCH disaffiliated from the network to become the first independent television station in Canada.

A short time later, Soble converted the former Kenmore Theatre on King Street West into TV11's Telecentre and began building up his TV station's presence.

Soble, who died in 1966, had founded a broadcasting empire. Yet, he modestly insisted: "I don't really have any talent of my own, unless it's a knack for finding good people to run my businesses, and then leaving them alone."

In 1984, the television station's historic headquarters, a stately 1840s Georgian-style mansion, was linked with a modern, high-tech facility allowing the station to bring its operations under one roof.

In the area of sales and marketing, the station is taking an integrated approach towards solving its clients' problems and has branded itself as a dynamic and innovative media partner.

The station has launched a number of successful partnership campaigns for the Ontario Jockey Club and Heart and Stroke Foundation while sponsorships have included the Molson Indy. And, it has joined with Bell Mobility, Young Drivers of Canada and Canadian Tire in the Ontario Ministry of Transportation's Road Safety Partnership program.

By the mid-1990s, the station had grown to around 170 employees operating such facilities as a state-of-the-art broadcast centre; two microwave mobiles, three production studios, two TV production mobiles for remote productions, plus editing suites and post-audio facilities.

It's the station's employees, with their enthusiastic commitment to excellence, who have made the transition to ONtv successful, says Macdonald.

"Dedicated staff, propelled by personal, professional pride and the encouragement from committed viewers and community members, have worked long, hard hours during this wonderful transition period," asserts Macdonald.

"Dramatic shifts in the television industry made it a competitive necessity to expand the coverage area," he explains.

"It is most gratifying to see the hard work of so many dedicated individuals become a tangible reality."

▶
*Jim Macdonald, left, and Bryan Ellis are part of the team behind ONtv's success.*
– PHOTO BY DAVID GRUGGEN

*Success Stories*

# Ntv

# Stirling Print-All

Life's blackest moments can hide a wealth of living colour.

That's the belief of battle-scarred Bob Stirling, whose industry went through a disruptive, rapid evolution into digital colour output services.

The owner of Stirling Print-All could have followed others who hid from the whirlwind of change and avoided risky expenditures on expensive new digital technology. Instead, he invested heavily in the new technology, recognizing its potential for improving operations to provide a better, faster service to customers.

The gutsy move – which continues to pay impressive dividends – is the result of Stirling leading the industry and acting on a deeply ingrained business philosophy.

"Success often depends on openly embracing change, with all of its challenges," Stirling says in an interview at his King Street East, Hamilton headquarters.

"A negative challenge can be turned inside out and be viewed as a potentially beneficial opportunity to improve services in a cost-effective way," he adds.

"You just have to look for the opportunities that exist in every challenge."

Stirling looked. And he liked what he saw. He invested hundreds of thousands of dollars in the new technology.

By the early 1990s, digital colour output services accounted for fully 10 per cent of Stirling's business while the lion's share remained in traditional printing and binding services.

By the late 1990s, 30 per cent of his business was digital "and it'll likely hit 50 per cent by the year 2000," suggests Stirling, who lauds the technology's ability to output full-colour images direct from disk to meet on-demand, just-in-time, full-colour services required in today's marketplace.

Stirling finds the digital colour output technology is ideal for addressing short-run demands for brochures, manuals, newsletters and catalogues.

The company can receive a customer's advertising prototype via computer, then massage the information, provide imaging and send the completed digital image back to the customer, anywhere in the world, in a largely paperless creative process.

"Digital is very fast – virtually instant," explains Stirling, whose company stands out in the Greater Hamilton market as a print shop and full graphic design shop which has aggressively evolved into the field of digital services.

"With digital, our initial proof copy is an actual usable copy, not just a sample. It's the first copy of the order. It's all done electronically – and what you see is what you get, in living colour," he explains.

One of the keys to Stirling's success has been his ability to stay on top of the technological changes in the industry during decades of business life.

> "Success often depends on openly embracing change. You just have to look for opportunities that exist in every challenge."

In the mid-1960s, he was a 16-year-old employee of hardware distributor Wood Alexander when his hands first came in contact with printer's ink.

He learned to run a printing press, and became immersed in the printing business. Positions of press operator to branch manager of an instant print franchise followed.

Then, in 1974, Stirling took out a second mortgage on his home and went into business on his own, opening Stirling Print-All in a little shop on King Street East. By 1978, demand for his services resulted in the company moving down King Street to its current location of King East at West Avenue, boasting some 15,000 square feet of space.

Even then, the industry was evolving. "In order to get print jobs, we had to offer creative services," he recalls, noting long-standing customer demand for one-stop creative/printing services.

Coupled with new technology, Stirling cites people as being vital to his success. "We wouldn't be where we are today if not for our well-connected team, our well-groomed core group of people who have had the vision and the willingness to embrace newer, better ways of doing things," says Stirling.

Today, Stirling employs a total of 38 people, including such core employees as his wife Mary, who oversees payroll and benefits; his brother Bill, sales manager; assistant, Cathy Miller; Frank Fursman, plant manager; Ron Wilkie, creative director; comptroller Sandra Scaletta; credit manager James Case; copy services manager Valerie Clark; and sales associates Nancy Gamble, Wendy Browning, Ian Wilkie and Jon Lazarowich.

With its diverse customer base crossing many economic sectors, the firm is one of the stronger performers in a struggling industry. Revenue has been growing at the rate of 10 per cent annually. Profit has been growing at 10-15 per cent annually.

Driving this impressive growth is Stirling's willingness – make that insistence – on working well beyond any 9-5 day. He's an exacting professional who lives, eats and breathes his business. Long hours are a necessary part of Stirling's relentless efforts to achieve greater levels of business success.

A self-confessed workaholic, Stirling literally catches the competition napping by starting his work days at 5 a.m. "I've found this quiet time of the day can also be the most productive part of the day," explains Stirling, who routinely completes an astonishing amount of work while most of us are still asleep.

But after 14-hour days, he makes sure the evenings are spent with his wife and children. He's also a strong supporter of youth, arts and music programs in the Hamilton community.

Although the market for print and creative services has been growing only slowly, Stirling has achieved much of his ongoing growth by capturing a larger share of the market and displacing lesser competitors. By the year 2000 he expects to launch storefront digital print centres.

"Digital is certainly our growth area," and I believe we're positioned right for the future," asserts Stirling.

"We still tell people," he says: "Put us to the test and we'll come through with flying colours."

▶

*Bob Stirling has invested heavily in new technology to keep his company on top.*
*– PHOTO BY DAVID GRUGGEN*

*Stirling Print-All*

*Success* 85 *Stories*

# David Gruggen Photography

By now, you already *know* why David Gruggen is a worthy Success Stories profile. As this book's principal photographer, his talent is showcased in living colour, page after gorgeous page.

His captivating pictorials, his sweeping panoramic scenes, his rich portraits of successful business people are visually arresting and inspiring.

With his sharp eye for composition, Gruggen, 41, is drawing an appreciative audience through his sense of drama, his technical expertise, his knack for always getting the right picture.

The head of Hamilton-based David Gruggen Photography has seen his professional touch displayed at exhibitions and in brochures, posters and books.

Gruggen's work has won him hundreds of corporate clients, including Dofasco, Wescam, Procter & Gamble, M.A. Henry, ONtv, Ernst & Young, Orlick Industries, McMaster University, Mohawk College, Lakeport Brewing, McKeil Marine, Elco Home Fashions, Nova Analytical Systems, Brown Boggs, Cambridge Group, Copley Group, Hamilton-Wentworth Economic Development Department and The Hamilton Spectator.

He was a featured photographer for the city's sesquicentennial coffee table book Hamilton – It's Happening. And, he was named as the official photographer of the G7 Summit when political leaders from the world's seven richest nations met in Hamilton in the mid-1990s.

Choosing Gruggen to supply the book's illustrative component, was a comfortable decision that wasn't based solely on this photographer's proven talents.

I first came across this gentle giant of a shutterbug over 20 years ago when we were both Mohawk College students in the mid-1970s.

While taking Broadcast Journalism at the college, I discovered a stronger love for print journalism. While he was taking Television Arts, Gruggen discovered a stronger love for still photography.

We both drifted to the college student newspaper, The Phoenix. There, the head photographer David Gruggen joined editor Michael B. Davie and photographer Philippa Cleave, now Philippa Davie.

My future wife and I both found in Gruggen, a dedicated professional who excelled under pressure and happily filled the paper with great photos.

"I love photography," Gruggen asserts, somewhat unnecessarily at a 1997 meeting with myself and fellow Mohawk graduate, Bruno Ruberto, Success Stories publisher and BRaSH Publishing Inc. president.

"But ever since I was three years old, I wanted to be a TV cameraman," Gruggen confides over a pub lunch that has the three of us recollecting our college days.

"When I took the three-year television course at Mohawk, I had to meet the requirement of buying a still camera to learn about composition," he adds.

> "I like working for myself, setting my own hours, being my own boss. I can't think of anything else I'd rather do."

"I didn't really want to buy a camera. But I did – and I was hooked."

Following his stint with the college newspaper, Gruggen worked for Global Television as part of a crew video taping the antics of Second City's Andrea Martin, Catherine O'Hara, Dave Thomas, Eugene Levy, Joe Flaherty and the late John Candy. He also filmed Wintario draws, building his lighting, set-ups and location photography expertise.

But it wasn't long before Gruggen gravitated to the station's public relations department where he again became immersed in still photography.

Staff cutbacks at Global Television in the late 1970s found Gruggen shooting for such publications as Hamilton Magazine and The Burlington Gazette.

Then, Gruggen became adept at taking product photos as staff photographer for South-western Communications, since renamed Corporate Image.

He applied this experience to starting his own studio in 1980 in a building he continues to own on Glen Road in the Westdale community. He initially ran Procter & Gamble's audio-visual department before branching out to include a lengthy list of corporate clients.

David Gruggen Photography has a full studio, full service colour lab run by lab manager Ray Durritt, dry mounting and laminating services, digital enhancements, photo restorations and photographic back-lit transparencies for trade shows, with guaranteed quality and delivery times.

Gruggen also has a computerized office cost-accounting system and archival facilities – and he recently established a digital service bureau at his Westdale shop. "We're basically a one-stop photography shop with full in-house services," he explains. "I've been told I have enough equipment to set up a camera store. But I'm very technically oriented and very particular that I have the very best equipment I can use to get the best shot."

So far, Gruggen has managed to find that "best shot" thousand of times over a satisfying career that continues to find new clients and fans.

Gruggen's own sense of satisfaction is derived from the painstaking efforts he routinely employs to capture the most impressive photographs imaginable.

A consummate professional, striving for perfection, he sets high standards for his work – and then raises the standard with each new 'personal best'.

And his success has continued to build ever since he headed down that bumpy – but exhilarating – road to independence.

"Even when I was working for South-western, I wanted my own place," he says. "It seems to suit my personality. I like working for myself, setting my own hours, being my own boss, making a living as an industrial-commercial photographer."

Whenever he can get a break from his hectic schedule, Gruggen likes to head out to the cottage with his wife Dorothy and eight-year-old son Christopher, who has already caught the photography bug and plans to follow in his dad's footsteps.

"The work days can be quite long," Gruggen admits, "but I also can't think of anything else I'd rather do. I'm still hooked on photography."

▶
*David Gruggen first picked up a camera as a college student some 20 years ago. Today, he's still focussed and continues to be one of our top photographers.*

# David Gruggen Photography

*Success* 87 *Stories*

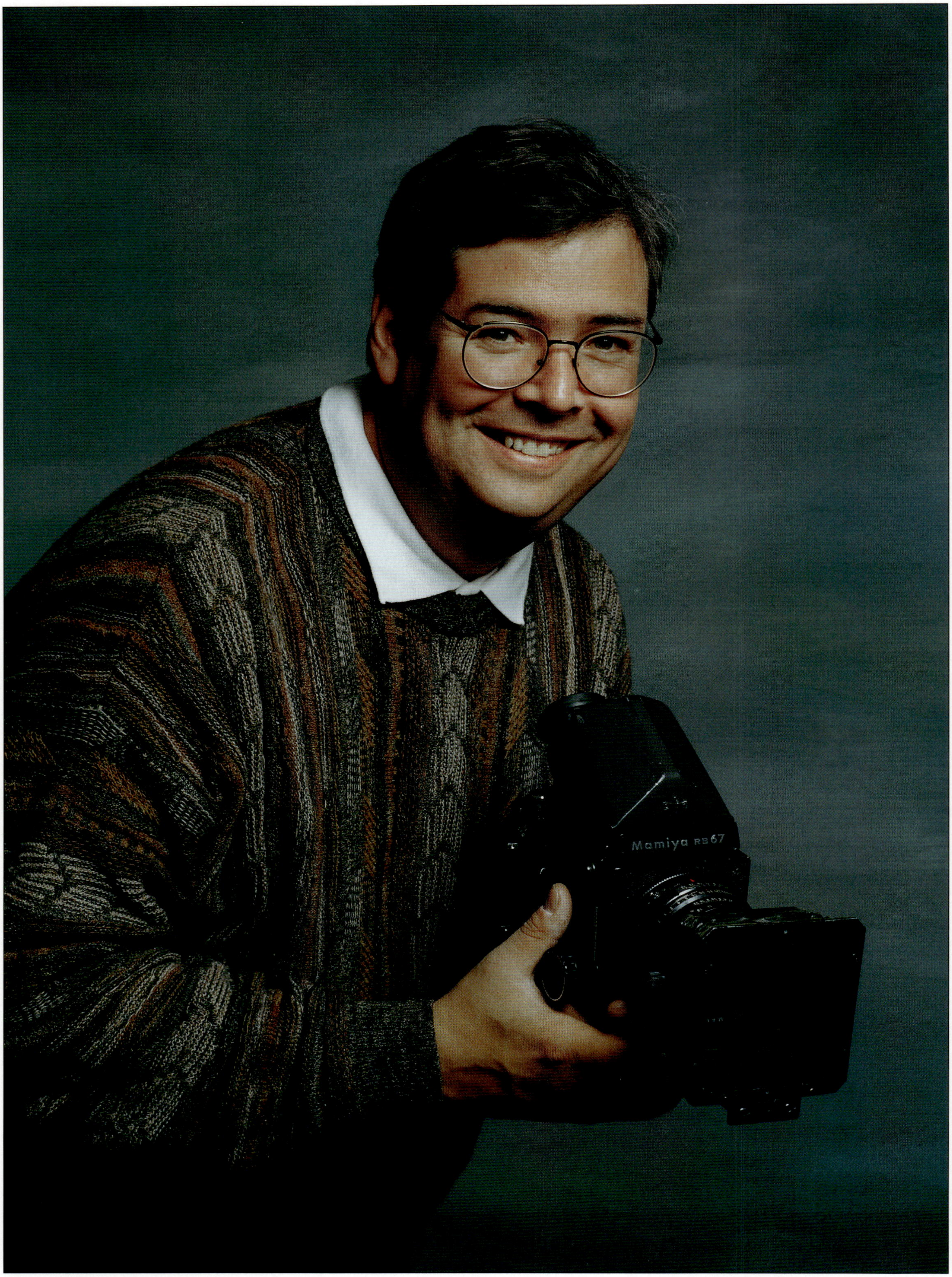
Mamiya RB67

# CHAPTER 7

# *Service Providers*

# Service Providers

The service sector. This outdated, catch-all phrase was once used to encompass everything that wasn't manufacturing.

It included everything from restaurants to hospitals to auto repair shops and other service-oriented businesses.

But explosive growth in an array of services, including the introduction of newly created services, led to a realization that there were, in fact, many services sectors which together account for at least half of the Canadian economy.

It's been said that the health care services sector now employs more people in Hamilton than the steel industry.

This shift in emphasis is felt everywhere, including the Greater Hamilton region which has found a promising source of new jobs and investment in services. And the range and number of services is growing.

"We're seeing tremendous growth in the various services sectors," asserts Neil Everson, manager of business development for Hamilton-Wentworth Economic Development Department.

"You need a strong manufacturing sector to have a strong services sector and that's certainly the case here," says Everson. "We have a strong and vibrant manufacturing sector – and this has given us a strong and rapidly growing services sector," he adds.

Everson says a rise or decline in the auto industry soon affects other manufacturing sectors and ultimately spills over into the various services sectors. "It's all tied in together," he points out. "If one sector sneezes, the other catches cold."

The growth of services is fueled by a growing trend towards specialization, offers Lee Kirkby, the former executive director of the Hamilton and District Chamber of Commerce.

"You'll often find the more individually focused employment is in the service fields," says Kirkby, "because that's where personal expertise is being bought and sold. The rising number of consulting jobs, computer experts and technical experts is evidence of the growing demand for certain types of expertise."

Kirkby also cites the combination of downsizing traditional employers and personal computer usage for creating a new environment receptive to individuals offering specialized services.

"It's a whole lot easier to operate as a sole proprietor now," Kirkby observes, "because technology has in large part eliminated the need for a traditional office and support structure to perform certain tasks. All you need is a personal computer and a telephone and you're in business."

He points to an explosion of home-based businesses as the most obvious sign of this new, nurturing environment for service-oriented sole proprietors. "It wasn't long ago," he says, "that it was considered quite unusual to work out of your home."

"It was assumed that someone working out of their home was unemployed or struggling or wasn't doing well enough to afford a proper office," adds Kirkby. "A home business address was looked on as bush league, not to be taken too seriously. Today, that stigma is no longer there."

He explains that the sheer numbers of home-based businesses, also a leading source of new chamber members, are making these predominantly service-oriented enterprises an accepted part of commercial life.

And while computers have made more businesses possible, the technology itself has generated more jobs, he observes.

"The big corporations and even the home-based businesses all tend to be utilizing computer technology," he adds, "and this has created new opportunities for people who manage, maintain and install computer technology."

Kirkby's comment brings to mind Micro Aide, a home-based business specializing in computer purchasing and system installation, needs evaluation, and custom programming.

Run by proprietors Bernd Grupe and Ron Weber, this highly reputable, Ancaster-based business is often going full-tilt to keep up with demand for its expertise and personal computer services.

The rise of Micro Aide and other such computer-oriented consulting companies is a function of the Information Age, our current era in which telephones, cell phones and personal computers are being co-opted into telecommunication systems.

Household PCs are more powerful than the old mainframe computers and the most valuable commodity is information itself.

"It's all part of a fundamental shift in our economy," Kirkby agrees. "Information and knowledge are more important now than ever before. And people who can offer services related to information and knowledge are in demand. The services part of the economy is growing rapidly."

With this, Kirkby pauses for moment to ponder the validity of phrases such as "services sectors," when describing the headlong shift into specialized services.

"Terms such as hard goods, soft goods, services and products have less meaning now because they've become cloudy and interchangeable," he considers with a shrug. "Software, for example, can be a service as much as a product."

And, Kirkby cites the growing demand for specialized niche services. "Most people are extremely busy at being productive, trying to generate an income, and they don't have the time, let alone the expertise, to take care of everything that needs taking care of in their lives," he explains. "And, so we turn to others who do have the time and expertise."

This trend, according to Kirkby, is in turn fuelling the growth of thousands of service-oriented businesses accounting for thousands of jobs across Canada.

A growing emphasis on high-quality, comprehensive services has led many service-oriented firms to focus sharply on offering as much value and variety as they possibly can.

This desire to be the best is reflected in many service-oriented companies, including the rapidly growing CARSTAR chain of automotive body shops, the very successful Mr. Mugs chain

> "We have a strong and vibrant manufacturing sector – and this has given us a strong and rapidly growing services sector."

*Success Stories*

# Service Providers

*Service with a smile at the five-star Sheraton Hamilton Hotel.*
*– PHOTO BY DAVID GRUGGEN*

of coffee and baked goods shops, and London Telecom, the highly innovative provider of long distance telephone services.

An imaginative – and effective approach – is also taken by Dr. Roland Estrabillo's dental practice, while fellow dentist Dr. Kevin Cooke emphasizes the impact a great smile can have on success.

His wife, chiropractor Dr. Catherine Cooke, employs a holistic approach to helping patients feel as well as humanly possible.

This focus on sound health as a major prerequisite to success is also found at International Family Fitness. This popular health club is successfully reaching out to a broader clientele with its equal emphasis on health and fitness.

All of these firms are listed in the directory at the back of this book for ready reference. We take a closer look at these examples of great service firms in a series of profiles, next.

*Success Stories*

# Dr. Roland Estrabillo

For Dr. Roland Estrabillo, success is constantly earned – and learned.

Although he's been a professional dentist for more than a decade, Estrabillo vows he'll never leave the learning mode. He's maintaining the role of student, continuing his life-long education, selecting mentors from dentistry and other fields to give him guidance.

I caught up with Estrabillo at his Upper Wentworth Street office in the summer of 1997. He had just spent his vacation time completing a gruelling, University of Toronto intravenous sedation certification course featuring nine straight 10-hour days and three exams.

Of his exhausting regimen, Estrabillo admits he "only slept about five hours."

"But if I want to keep up – I have to do this," he adds.

And, Estrabillo is determined to keep up in the rapidly evolving field of dentistry. He attends monthly seminars and he has also invested heavily in new computer equipment, technology, plus materials and methodologies to ensure that his practice succeeds at treating patients quickly and efficiently.

For example, his recent I-V sedation certification means he can comfortably sedate patients for longer periods while he performs cosmetic dentistry or full-mouth reconstructive surgery.

Although general family dentistry still accounted for 75 per cent of his practice caseload in the mid-1990s, Estrabillo was concentrating more on full-mouth reconstructive dentistry as a growing, and satisfying, part of his work.

"After the orthodontist and periodontist have treated the patient, I perform bridge work, teeth implants, crowns, veneers and cosmetic improvements to the patient's teeth," he explains.

"We've cut the time needed for a crown to just half an hour from an hour, so the patient is more comfortable."

Estrabillo notes that this full-mouth reconstruction, comprehensive dentistry can improve chewing efficiency, enhance the functioning of the jaw, save teeth and "actually make people look younger with whiter, rearranged, straighter teeth which support the mouth better."

He's also intent on making his office, himself and his entire staff as financially successful as possible.

Acting on the advice of former dentist and mentor Paul Bass, Estrabillo invests a portion of the practice's profit in mutual funds on behalf of each employee.

"Financial independence is a goal – so is providing the highest level of care," he notes. And, Estrabillo is proving the two go hand-in-hand: The investment plan has boosted already-high staff morale, creating a contagious enthusiasm spread from employees to patients who enjoy their visit enough to refer friends and family.

> "I have a number of mentors because I like learning something from people who have achieved success."

Estrabillo is integrating financial planning as a component of the mainly clinical, twice-monthly seminars that he holds to share product and methodology information with other dentists.

Another new component concerns the inter-relationship between dental practice and laboratory. This component is based on the work of Estrabillo's wife Maria, who operates her own on-site laboratory. She works as a technician, performing lab work for crowns, bridges and veneers.

Roland Estrabillo arrived in Canada from the Philippines in 1980 at age 20.

After graduating in 1987 from the University of Toronto with a degree in dentistry, he set up his practice on Upper Wentworth Street in a strip mall opposite Lime Ridge Mall.

Building his practice from scratch, Estrabillo was attending 6,000 to 7,000 patients by the mid-1990s.

By the early 1990s, he had outgrown his strip mall location and had relocated to renovated offices at his former home, also on Upper Wentworth Street. He's now contemplating opening a second office on the East Mountain to accommodate his growing practice.

Fuelling this impressive growth are referrals from satisfied patients who appreciate the extra care Estrabillo takes to make their visit pleasant – and brief.

And he's grateful for the input, advice and support received from mentors, fellow dentists and friends from all walks of life who have helped him overcome problems and achieve new levels of success in a demanding, time-consuming career.

"I have a number of mentors because I like learning something from people who have achieved success," says Estrabillo.

"I've learned from other doctors and I've taken courses regularly throughout my career. I copied a lot of other dentists' better techniques and added some of my own – and put it all together to share with others," he explains.

"Success is never something you achieve all by yourself," he adds.

"It's when you learn from others and share your own experiences that you improve in the process. Everyone benefits from this type of sharing."

That sharing process takes place during the seminars Estrabillo hosts to pass on to other dentists some of the efficient, time-saving techniques he's picked up during a cumulative, shared-learning experience spanning his full career.

And he is quick to attribute the success of his busy practice to his staff of 12, including a hygienist, support staff, and fellow dentists Dr. Nona Barrientos, Dr. Alex Gonzales and Dr. Carlana Midence.

"My staff is the best in the world," he asserts. "Without them, I could not have achieved anything that I have achieved."

"They play a big role in our success. They run my office and they take very good care of our patients. We do the best job we can and we try to have fun," he adds. "We all work together here."

"If my fellow workers are looked after well, you can bet they'll be the best co-workers you could possibly have," he says.

"High morale means that they perform really well. That's good for the patient – and for the success of the business."

▶
*Dr. Roland Estrabillo makes sure that his staff shares in his business success.*
– PHOTO BY DAVID GRUGGEN

*Success Stories*

# Dr. Roland Estrabillo

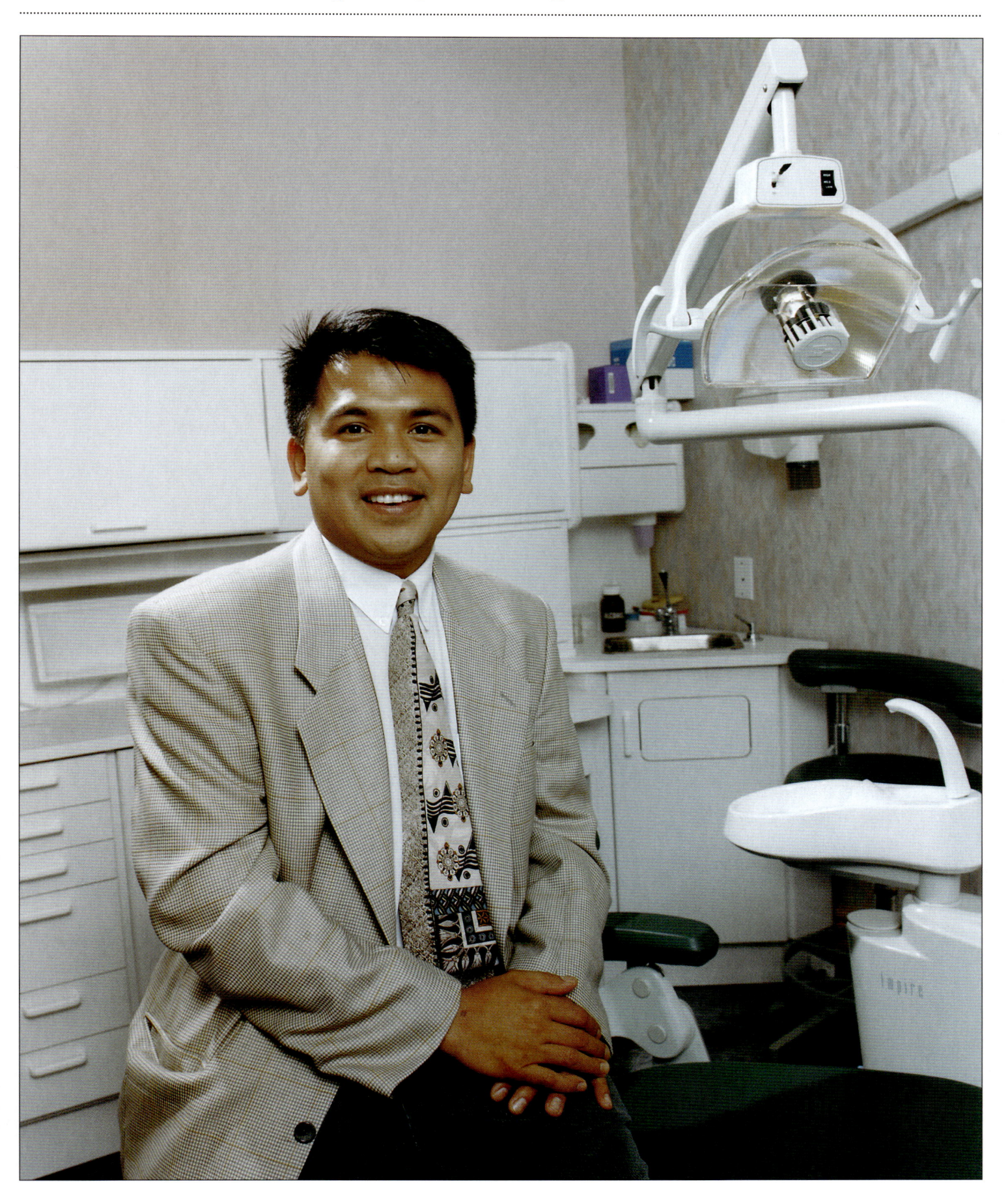

Success Stories

# Dr. Kevin Cooke

A smile can sometimes turn failure into success.

That sudden flash of white beams an instant message of friendly, self-assured confidence. Smiles are associated with success: Winners smile; losers don't.

A great smile wins people over, puts them at ease, helps makes business deals succeed. White teeth denote health, happiness, youthful vitality, sound self-esteem.

Conversely, discoloured teeth send out a message of ill-health, decay, perhaps low self-esteem. They lead to embarrassment, an erosion of self-confidence and self-conscious efforts to avoid smiling – with predictable results. The smiles become infrequent and ineffective.

To understand the importance of a simple smile, ask yourself, all other things being equal, are you more likely to buy a car from a smiling, confident salesman who seems genuinely happy to see you? Or would you rather hand your money to an unsmiling man with bad teeth?

Simply put, a great smile makes a great deal of difference, in business and in life.

Dr. Kevin Cooke is a Hamilton dentist who plays a leading role in creating great smiles. Cooke provides a full range of dental care. But the 39-year-old dentist specializes in aesthetic, cosmetic dentistry, placing an emphasis on making teeth look as attractive as possible.

"An improvement in self-esteem often follows an improvement in the appearance of teeth," says Cooke, at his 2,200-square-foot Garth Street dental offices where he's assisted by a staff of six in providing dental and patient education services.

"Aesthetic dentistry is certainly my main area of interest," adds the innovative, progressive dentist, who invested $50,000 in the spring of 1997 in state-of-the-art, laser-whitening equipment. And aesthetic dentistry complements Cooke's other professional passion: life-long learning.

Born and raised in Hamilton, Cooke attended Westdale high school and proved an avid student, winning the J. W. Bell Outstanding Student Award. His interest in learning continued at the College of Wooster, at Wooster, Ohio.

"After about two years of studying chemistry at the undergraduate level, I started looking at career opportunities, primarily in health care fields," he recalls.

Interested in obtaining an accurate impression of life in the medical field, Cooke decided to observe his family doctor and dentist for a day. It was an eye-opening experience.

"I found the life of a doctor to be a horrifying experience," Cooke says. "He was up at the crack of dawn performing surgery and he worked until late at night."

In contrast, Cooke found the dentist worked a 9-5 day, enjoyed his worklife and still had time for a family life. Best of all, dentistry was constantly changing. It would allow Cooke to pursue his interest in life-long learning.

> "I wanted something that would be satisfying yet challenging and constantly evolving. And, dentistry provided all of this."

"I wanted something that would be satisfying yet challenging and constantly evolving," he explains. "And, dentistry provided all of this," he adds. "It's not only challenged me, it's practically been my nemesis. Continuing education in dentistry isn't just valuable, it's mandatory."

Cooke completed his third year at Wooster, earning a Bachelor of Arts in Chemistry. He then earned his degree in dentistry at Case Western Reserve University at Cleveland, Ohio, in 1984.

On completing seven years of education in the United States, Cooke returned to Hamilton where his family has deep community roots.

His younger brother, Terry Cooke, is Hamilton-Wentworth regional chairman. Their father, Frank Cooke Jr., is superintendent of schools for Hamilton Mountain, with the Hamilton school board.

Their grandfather, Frank Cooke Sr., was general manager of the HSR and Canada Coach Lines.

Their uncle, Richard Cooke, is manager of operations planning at Stelco Inc. And Kevin Cooke's wife, Dr. Catherine Cooke, is a successful chiropractor.

After a few years of working in another dentist's office, Kevin Cooke established his own practice in 1987 with 600-700 patients. The practice would enjoy steady, moderate growth over the next 10 years. He continues to build his clientele and is contemplating moving to larger quarters in the Meadowlands area of Ancaster.

A major turning point in Cooke's career occurred in the spring of 1994 when he took part in the aesthetic dentistry program at the Baylor College of Dentistry at Dallas, Texas.

The prestigious program emphasized hands-on dentistry, with participants bringing along their own patients to undergo aesthetic dental treatments.

Cooke was definitely up for the challenge. Operating on Laura Doucette, a sales agent with the Hamilton offices of NBR Realty, he replaced all of her silver fillings with tooth-coloured restorations – also known as invisible fillings.

Her front teeth were also given a porcelain veneer, a dramatic improvement. Doucette's smiling image can be found on Cooke's office walls – and her own business cards and advertising.

Baylor honoured Cooke with an award for his exemplary, comprehensive aesthetic restorative work – and invited the young dentist back that fall to help teach the program. Cooke's reputation for excellence in aesthetic dentistry was made.

Through his work at Baylor, he was put in touch with leading American cosmetic dentists who introduced him to a number of the time-tested, high-tech dentistry devices he has adopted. "I try to stay close to the edge in dentistry – but with technology that has already been proven in thousands of clinical trials," he says.

Cooke makes regular use of air and particle abrasion instruments which are used in lieu of a drill for many fillings. These instruments lack the noise, heat and chattering-vibration of drills – and can often be used without freezing the mouth.

Cooke also uses cosmetic imaging technology employing computer-generated simulated images to show patients what their teeth would look like after an aesthetic procedure.

He also uses intraoral cameras. With a lens fitted at the end of a pen-shaped device, Cooke moves this wand around the inside of the mouth of a patient, who can watch it all on a TV screen.

# Dr. Kevin Cooke

"It works wonders with the most skeptical patients," Cooke says, "because they can see for themselves exactly where there are any cracks or cavities in their teeth."

And, there's the argon laser technology.

"The advantage of laser technology doesn't end with its ability to dramatically whiten teeth," asserts Cooke, who is one of only a handful of dentists in Ontario known to be using lasers.

"Lasers can be used very effectively for hardening light-activated tooth fillings," he explains. "A laser can harden a filling in five seconds instead of the 30 seconds required by the old technology. Lasers can also be used in minor gum surgery."

While such technological marvels are costly investments, Cooke is determined to continue adopting the best in proven dentistry advancements to better serve his appreciative patients.

"In the end, they're only tools," he says, "but I like to have the best tools available – to do the best work I possibly can."

▲
*Dr. Kevin Cooke activates an argon laser utilized in the whitening of teeth and the hardening of filling materials.*
– PHOTO BY DAVID GRUGGEN

*Success Stories*

# Dr. Catherine Cooke

In 1969, an anxious eight-year-old Catherine Glady stood at her mother's bedside. The recent birth of Catherine's younger brother Fred had left her mother Carol bed-ridden with chronic lower back pain, despite repeated treatments by conventional physicians.

This young girl would one day become successful chiropractor Dr. Catherine Cooke. But her mother's painful plight in the late '60s remains a poignant memory.

"When you're a child, you think of your parents as being invincible," Cooke says. "It was devastating to see my mother so sore she could hardly get out of bed."

But the situation changed dramatically after the Glady family turned to a chiropractor, an unusual step at a time when chiropractic procedures were dismissed in some quarters as quackery.

"This woman chiropractor adjusted my mom's back and had her out of bed in a matter of weeks," recollects Cooke.

"I was amazed," she adds, "at how well this chiropractor helped my mother's body to heal itself. I was tremendously grateful, and I was really impressed."

So impressed, that the experience was forever ingrained in her consciousness.

Cooke went on to excel academically in high school, winning several awards for scholastic excellence.

As she approached her final year in high school, she was interested in a career in the health care field, but was unsure which particular discipline to pursue.

"I discussed this with my mother who reminded me of her experience with a chiropractor," she says.

"As I remembered the importance of that experience, and its impact on my life, I knew I'd like to investigate becoming a chiropractor and help others."

"The more I looked into the philosophy of the chiropractic profession, the more fascinating I found it," adds Cooke.

"It's a natural, holistic approach which provides tremendous assistance, but lets the body heal itself," she explains.

In 1980, as a step towards an eventual chiropractic doctorate, she enrolled in Human Kinetics – the study of anatomy and the body in motion – at the University of Guelph. She found her studies offered "a fascinating look at the body's ability to rapidly adapt to changes in physical and environmental conditions."

One experiment involved monitoring subjects on a stationary bicycle in an enclosed chamber. As the temperature in the chamber was increased, the subject's body quickly adapted in a complex fashion. The degree of stress noted on the heart was tremendous.

In 1982, Cooke was accepted at The Canadian Memorial Chiropractic College in Toronto. She graduated Magna Cum Laude with a Doctorate of Chiropractic in 1986 and was chosen as Intern of the Year by the clinic doctors.

> *I remove the obstacles to healing and let the body do its own repair work. Nothing works as well as the body left on its own.*

Dr. Catherine Glady set up practice on Church Street in Toronto, next to a fitness club in the heart of the city's gay community. It was a baptism by fire.

"Beyond treating a lot of sports injuries, I did a lot of work with AIDS patients," recalls Dr. Catherine Cooke in an interview at her clinic at Garth and Garrow streets on Hamilton Mountain.

"At my Toronto clinic, unless someone told me they were not HIV positive, I could usually assume they were, the AIDS epidemic was that severe," she adds.

"I treated many full-blown AIDS patients, some emaciated and others with facial and other tumors," she says of this learning experience.

"These people were under incredible stress because they were either ill themselves or coping with the fact that people they loved were dying," Cooke explains.

"Our main focus was to try to boost the immune system by enabling the nervous system to function better," she adds. "The body has an innate ability to heal itself and chiropractic adjustments allow it to function at a more optimum level."

Cooke says that adjustments primarily decrease nerve irritation by relieving pressure on the nerves entering the central nervous system when this pressure results from misalignments of the vertebrae.

The spinal column, she explains, is made up of 24 bones and protects the spinal chord which acts like a tree trunk, branching out into a myriad of nerve branches which exit between vertebrae bones and become smaller and more profuse as they move further away from the spinal column. These nerves travel to all parts of the body and allow the brain to communicate with all of the cells in the body. Therefore, "back problems" can manifest themselves as problems with more distant parts of the body.

"Chiropractic adjustments decrease nerve irritation so information is facilitated along the nerve lines in a process that affects the whole body," Cooke elaborates. "I'm just enabling the nervous system to function appropriately, by adjusting vertebrae to relieve irritation and pressure. By removing obstacles to healing we enable the body to do its own repair work."

Cooke notes that some patients have reported a loss or reduction of headaches and allergy symptoms after chiropractic adjustments. The adjustments removed nerve irritation that had contributed to hyperactive nerves and hypersensitivity to certain foods or pollen.

"Once the nerves are functioning properly, they may not over-react to the same degree to normal environmental agents and the body can regain its ability to respond correctly," she explains.

And it's vital to solve problems, not just treat the symptoms, she adds.

"Too often, people try to mask pain with drugs. I always ask: 'Why is this nerve yelling, what warning is it giving us?' I remove the obstacles to healing and let the body do its own repair work."

"Nothing works as well as the human body left on its own," Cooke states.

"It's designed perfectly and it usually works well unless it's overwhelmed by nerve irritation or worn down by physical and emotional stress. A chiropractic adjustment is just a process that enables a body to look after itself. It's just enhancing a body's own ability to perform."

While visiting her grandmother's house in Hamilton in 1987 to learn how to bake pies, Cooke was introduced to Dr. Kevin

# Dr. Catherine Cooke

*Dr. Catherine Cooke demonstrates her technique on office manager Veronica Allen.*
– PHOTO BY DAVID GRUGGEN

Cooke, a dentist, out walking his dog.

The two medical professionals later married, with the young chiropractor accepting Cooke as her married name. "And Kevin talked me into moving to Hamilton," Cooke recalls with a smile.

Her grandparents are now her oldest patients. Both are in their 90s and are remarkably fit for their age.

Dr. Catherine Cooke's Chiropractic Office opened in the fall of 1988. The four-person practice remains a going concern, run from the beginning by office manager Veronica Allen.

"Our whole staff is a team," Cooke says, "and our team determines what the patient's experience with us will be like."

"Our team creates an environment conducive to healing for the patient," she adds. "It's a very loving atmosphere. I sometimes think people come here as much for the hugs as the adjustments."

This caring approach is generating considerable interest and support.

The clinic has long been one of the busiest clinics in the province. Cooke is contemplating bringing in another chiropractor to share the workload.

Most chiropractic adjustments are performed in just minutes and objective indicators, to measure improvement, are recorded by Cooke, who belongs to a 14-member chiropractic group sharing information to improve the profession.

"A real benefit is that the patient gets a better understanding of their body," says the busy, holistic chiropractor, who rollerblades, kayaks, climbs, scuba dives and runs in long distance races to maintain the strong physical condition needed to keep up with her demanding practice.

"Knowledge is power and the power to look after yourself better is extremely valuable," explains Cooke, clearly driven by a sense of mission. "If the source of someone's pain is removed, their quality of life is enhanced as is the quality of the lives of those around them, thus creating a ripple effect on the whole community."

"My work is almost addictive. That's how much satisfaction I get from making a difference in people's lives."

"Why wait until you're not feeling well before getting a needed chiropractic adjustment?" Cooke asks.

"Taking a proactive approach to health helps us feel as well as humanly possible," she says. "And that enables each of us to better fulfill our own mission in life."

*Success Stories*

# Mr. Mugs Coffee & Donuts

The rain beat against the coffee shop's windows as Paul Cleave glanced outside at the downpour, cradling a hot cup of coffee in his large hands.

It was the mid-1980s. Cleave, owner of a small excavating and construction firm, tried to recall how many times rain had forced him to stop work in the 10 years he'd had his business.

His thoughts were interrupted as a pair of wet construction workers hurriedly entered the crowded coffee shop. The men quickly joined a line of damp patrons eager to warm up with a cup of coffee.

The entrepreneur returned his attention to the window. Through the rain-streaked glass, he saw the blurred images of three other men running towards the shop. It looks like nobody is doing any business today, Cleave smiled to himself. Nobody, he realized, except the coffee shop.

The young businessman looked around the busy shop. Every seat was occupied.

There was a steady line-up for coffee. And, the door kept opening and closing as patron after patron placed coffee orders.

"I saw a real business opportunity," Cleave recalls in a fall, 1997 interview, "because the coffee shops seemed to be a strong business."

"Being in construction, I frequented these shops a lot," he adds, "and they always seemed to be busy, rain or shine."

Cleave enjoyed being in business for himself. But after a decade of construction work, he was ready to try something new.

In late 1986, he opened the first-ever Mr. Mugs Coffee and Donuts store, at Grand Bend, Ontario.

The name was derived by reversing the words: coffee mugs. The store adopted a company colour scheme, and a Mr. Mugs mascot was concocted in the form of a giant sheepdog cartoon character.

Cleave initially started his Mr. Mugs business with a partner, Ron Hewitt, and the two launched their fledgling firm with their own funds and borrowed money.

From the beginning, Mr. Mugs targeted a niche market: smaller communities or neighbourhoods that weren't already awash with competing coffee and donut shops. In Grand Bend, they found one of those under-serviced communities – and many more would follow.

"We didn't mind if there was some competition," Cleave points out. "But there didn't seem much point in going into neighbourhoods that already had a coffee shop on every corner."

Mr. Mugs opened three more stores the following spring, at Arnprior, Brantford and Caledonia, giving the firm a total of four company-owned stores in its first six months of operation.

"Then we franchised these four stores," Cleave says, "and a fifth store, in Ottawa, opened a little later as our first store that was a franchise location from the start."

> *Our coffee shop became the place to go, the community focal point, the meeting place where friends and neighbours got together.*

"Our goal from the beginning was to franchise locations as much as possible while having some company-owned stores as well," he says, noting that locations are selected carefully. The criteria includes exposure and visibility, adequate parking, easy accessibility and proximity to busy traffic flow. The nearness of competitors is much less of a concern, especially if the site meets all of the selection criteria.

While building the Mr. Mugs chain, Cleave and Hewitt also founded a couple of Desperadoes taverns. But Cleave was simply more comfortable with the Mr. Mugs chain. The partnership dissolved in 1995 with Hewitt holding the taverns and Cleave assuming sole ownership of the Mr. Mugs coffee and donut stores chain.

By 1997, the Mr. Mugs chain had grown to 20 stores, five of them company-owned locations. Each store averages $400,000 in annual sales. The company's annual revenue exceeds $8 million.

In addition to the original four stores, Mr. Mugs has added two more stores to Brantford, bringing the total to three in that community. There are also Mr. Mugs stores in Port Dover, Wawa, Hagersville, Acton, Kitchener, Port Elgin and Dundas, plus two in Hamilton.

And, there are five Mr. Mugs stores in Eastern Ontario, mainly in communities which previously lacked a coffee shop.

"At that time, that area of Ontario was really under-serviced with coffee shops – so this was a strong opportunity," recalls Cleave, who often flies to the chain's more distant stores in his Cesna 182 aircraft.

Although new to these centres, it didn't take Mr. Mugs long to become a local landmark and part of each community's cultural fabric, Cleave notes.

"Some of the towns we'd go into, in Eastern Ontario and locally, would have a tavern or a family restaurant and some of the people would go to one or the other."

"But our coffee shop became the place everyone could go to," Cleave recalls with pride. "It became the community focal point, the meeting place where friends and neighbours got together."

"For example, in Hagersville and Acton, we were by ourselves as the only coffee shop so we became the local meeting place," he adds. "We try to encourage community involvement at our stores. We try to build a sense of community identity to be a part of their lives."

This has been achieved by posting community bulletin boards in some of his stores and by supporting local worthy causes. Among the charities sponsored are the Heart & Stroke Foundation, Easter Seals and Canadian Cancer Society.

And Cleave looks for this same sense of community in Mr. Mugs franchisees, along with a good sense of business, self-motivation and a cheerful attitude.

"By and large we're pretty happy with our franchisees," he says, adding "and I think they're pretty happy with us."

They should be: Buying into a Mr. Mugs franchise is possible at a fraction of what larger competitors charge.

Yet the franchisee is still serviced by many of the same suppliers and franchise benefits include training and chain-wide marketing and advertising support. The dream of running a franchise business has rarely been this accessible or affordable.

Being a Mr. Mugs franchisee also means being part of an innovative firm.

Mr. Mugs was the first coffee and donuts chain to broaden its menu with soups and sandwiches. It offers a full lunch counter array of foods, including

# Mr. Mugs Coffee & Donuts

bagels, muffins and flavoured gourmet coffees. And, it frequently holds contests offering prizes ranging from free coffees to free trips for two to Hollywood.

Cleave anticipates continued growth at a moderate rate for the Mr. Mugs chain, with the addition of just a few new stores each year, primarily in under-serviced areas where Mr. Mugs stores can shine in their dual role as busy coffee shop and community meeting place.

"The business is constantly evolving," Cleave explains.

"Regular coffee and donuts are still popular. But we'd like to be known as a coffee shop that also sells bagels, donuts muffins, soups and sandwiches."

"People's eating habits are changing," he notes, "so it's important to offer a wider selection to keep up with consumer demands – and continue to be a part of their lives, rain or shine."

▲
*Paul Cleave, with daughter Amy, one of the smiling faces greeting customers at the Mr. Mugs store in Dundas.*
– PHOTO BY DAVID GRUGGEN

# International Family Fitness Centres

**H**is company's growing bottom line doesn't impress Gene Kay.

The co-owner of International Family Fitness Centres and The One Club – Women's Fitness, gets more satisfaction from shrinking bottoms, waistlines and love handles.

"Profit is still essential – otherwise we can't do a lot of the things we do," Kay explains. "But it's not our bottom line that motivates us – it's our primary goal of helping people improve their lives," he adds in an interview at the firm's corporate headquarters in Hamilton.

"Success for us is seeing someone start an exercise program, or a weight loss of 100 pounds or a 70-year-old as spry as a 35-year old. We promote what we subscribe to ourselves. If we didn't believe in this, if we were just another dollar-chasing company, we'd pack it in today."

Kay sounds like a man on a mission – and he is. Holding up some literature on the U.S. Surgeon General's 1996 Report on Physical Activity and Health, he notes that the last time this leading medical authority released a major report was the landmark pronouncement in 1962 which found smoking is harmful to your health.

Over 30 years later, there's the new landmark report. Its principal finding: Exercise isn't just good for you, it won't merely add years to your life, it's absolutely critical!

The report bluntly states a total lack of exercise is so harmful to your health, it's like smoking a pack of cigarettes a day.

For Kay, the report is an another confirmation he and partner, Mike Watson, are providing an important service and have been on the right track since opening their first fitness club in 1981.

Although their Champions chain of fitness clubs became famous, the name was changed to International Family Fitness in 1992 in an effort to clear away any misconceptions that the clubs were geared to super athletes. The new name reaches out to a wider clientele.

"The family concept is something we feel very strongly about. It's the primary reason for the name change from Champions," says Kay. "Our clubs are designed to offer world-class facilities and services at affordable family rates."

The average age of Family Fitness members is now 34, an increase of 10 years since the name change, notes Asim Iqbal, a chartered accountant, who joined the company in 1992 and is today a partner and Chief Financial Officer.

"Revenue has doubled in the past five years and we're using a planned approach to tap into the baby boomer market," adds Iqbal, who joined Kay for the interview.

Watson is where he can usually be found: at one of the fitness clubs, strolling between rows of treadmills and lifecycles.

> "We preach the total wellness concept. We truly measure our success by the number of people we've helped."

With a physique that still looks like it's carved out of stone, Watson, a former Mr. Canada, enjoys chatting with Family Fitness members ranging in age from late teens to early seventies.

"I can remember back in 1981 when Gene and I opened our first club on the East Mountain – even then I knew this was our future," Watson recalls.

"The success of our company was founded on the support of our members and the strength of our co-workers – many of our members have remained loyal to our company since 1981," adds the two-time National bodybuilding champion.

"It's really encouraging to walk through one of our clubs and see a retiree, at age 67, keeping fit with a positive attitude and a smile on their face," says Watson.

"That's the type of personal reward that makes us realize we're on the right track," adds Watson, a hands-on marketer who stresses the importance of taking a personal approach to working with members.

The company's winning approach is detailed in the critically acclaimed book Life is Good. Fitness Makes It Better! which Kay compiled and co-authored along with Watson and Mark Stonehouse, a personal trainer.

Muscle & Fitness magazine deemed the book a "must-read," while Canadian Press, The Hamilton Spectator and major newspapers across Canada have lauded the book for its "sensible approach to improving health."

This straightforward, informative and reader-friendly book makes it clear that remarkable improvements can be achieved by just about anyone with as little as 30 minutes of exercise daily.

Staffed by a total workforce of 140 employees, the clubs are spacious, spotless, reasonably priced and run by a professional and enthusiastic team who work with all members to ensure they receive the maximum enjoyment and benefit from their membership experience.

Family Fitness clubs have also played host to professional athletes, including members of the CFL Hamilton Tiger-Cats, AHL Bulldogs and NBA Toronto Raptors.

The American Thunderbirds aerial acrobatics squad has also exercised at their clubs. So has Canadian comic Tommy Chong of Cheech & Chong fame and music stars of the Juno Awards.

Already established operators of The One Club at Jackson Square, the company added the largest exclusively women's location in Canada: a 15,000-square-foot facility at Lime Ridge Mall.

Although it's hard to imagine where she has room for physical improvement, German-born super model Claudia Shiffer has trained at the downtown One Club, as has actress Geena Davis.

There's also a Family Fitness club on Barton Street East and the sprawling, 30,000-square-foot health club at South Hamilton Square at Upper James and Rymal Road.

The company is again poised for growth with plans to open an even larger facility – some 40,000 square feet – at a new location to be opened in 1998 near the Oakville-Mississauga border.

In addition to these half-dozen, company-owned clubs there is a vibrant 30,000-square-foot, state-of-the-art franchise location in Kitchener. And, there are plans to open several more company clubs over the next few years.

*Success Stories*

# International Family Fitness Centres

Voted six consecutive times by The Hamilton Spectator's readers as the area's best health club, Family Fitness maintains high standards of excellence and was nominated for 1995 Entrepreneur of the Year by the Bank of Montreal.

It's by far the largest club in the region and is one of the largest in Ontario with some 20,000 members, twice the number it had just five years ago.

Living up to their vision statement: "To enhance the quality of life of our members, and our community," the three partners believe in giving back to the community. They're strong supporters of Ontario Special Olympics and over 120 other worthy local causes. They also believe in exercise as the key to adding years to your life and life to your years.

"We preach the total wellness concept," Kay exclaims, "and we truly measure our success by the number of people we've helped. There's no secret to a healthier, longer life – it's exercise!"

▲
*Gene Kay, left, Mike Watson, centre, and Asim Iqbal all believe that exercise is the key to a longer and healthier life.*
– PHOTO BY DAVID GRUGGEN

*Success Stories*

# CarStar Automotive

Picture yourself at the side of a roadway. You've just had a collision with another vehicle. Fortunately nobody is badly injured. But your vehicle is severely damaged. The front end is crumpled and windows are shattered.

Still shaking from your narrow escape, you relate the details to the police.

But what about your vehicle?

You then remember to call Ontario Auto Collision CARSTAR.

With that one phone call, a tow truck is quickly dispatched, towing along with it a service vehicle you then drive home.

The tow truck takes your damaged car to a nearby CARSTAR location where video images of the damage are relayed via computer to the Claims Adjustment Centre and to your insurer. Repairs are rapidly authorized and under way.

In what seems like a very short time, your fully repaired car is delivered to you.

CARSTAR has virtually eliminated any confusion or repair delay following your accident. You're pleased, happy, perhaps even ready to become a new CARSTAR customer for life.

"We're in the catastrophe business," says Sam Mercanti, founding CEO of both Hamilton-based Ontario Auto Collision CARSTAR and CARSTAR Automotive Canada, which awards franchises to body shops meeting the firm's high ethical standards and qualifications.

"Every accident is somewhat traumatic because it's upsetting, unexpected, but your experience getting your car repaired should be as satisfying as possible," adds Mercanti in an interview at Canadian headquarters on Rymal Road.

"Our goal is to make you an apostle – you're so happy, you're bragging about our services to your friends and family."

Born in Italy but raised in Hamilton, Mercanti left school at age 17 to work as a detail man and later as a painter for his uncles Nardino and Guerino at Mercanti Brothers Autobody Shop.

When the city expropriated the brothers' Strachan Street location in 1970, the company moved to Gage Avenue North and was renamed Ontario Auto Collision.

With the new location came a new role for Sam Mercanti, then in his early 20s. He was put in charge of customer relations, running the front desk and also managing the business. And, he was soon made a partner with his two uncles and a third uncle, Anthony Mercanti.

At that time, the bulk of the company's business was coming from used car and warranty jobs and only 5 per cent from the insurance companies.

"I decided to go after the untapped insurance business and I met with brokers, agents and appraisers to assess their needs and earn their business," recalls Sam Mercanti, who also promoted franchising the company and introduced its famous pledge to do a "bang up job every time."

> *Our goal is to make you an apostle – you're so happy about our service you're bragging to your friends and family.*

In just two short years, Mercanti built up the insurance side of the business to exceed 50 per cent of revenue. By 1972, revenue exceeded $1 million. By the late 1970s it was $2 million.

With the famous "bang up" slogan, Mercanti had turned Ontario Auto Collision into a household name.

Then he went on to expand this name recognition, customer service and size of the company by strategically aligning OAC with CARSTAR, a U.S.-based collision repair franchise firm.

In the 1980s, Mercanti established Ontario Trucking Division for collision repairs to trucks and the company opened its $5 million auto centre on Rymal Road East in Hamilton.

By the mid-1990s, revenue rang in at $25 million and Mercanti was acting on a signed agreement with CARSTAR which has 360 locations in the U.S. Mercanti has the exclusive rights to open and license CARSTAR locations in Canada.

The insurance side now accounts for 90 per cent of revenue as insurance carriers increasingly rely on CARSTAR's integrity and dependability.

Mercanti has expanded "the trust factor" by using digital, computer-driven video imaging, allowing insurance appraisers to get a good look at damage without leaving their office.

The result: repairs are authorized and completed faster, with better quality than the average body shop – and with less inconvenience to consumers.

By 1997, the company boasted 50 locations, mainly in Ontario, with a few in Western Canada and Quebec.

Mercanti credits success to key people such as president Larry Jeffries; corporate location manager Remo Mercanti; chief information officer Cathy Puckering; and business solutions group director Dan Thompson. He also cites vice-presidents: Tony Mercanti, operations; Norm Angrove, sales; Sam Malatesta, marketing; Ruth Liebersbach, finance.

Also fuelling the company's growth is Mercanti's ongoing emphasis on working with the insurance industry to secure a larger share of the auto body market.

"Based on our reputation for honesty and integrity, insurance companies will automatically approve our repair claims in most instances, without involving an appraiser, notes Mercanti. "And that saves everyone time and money."

Mercanti is marketing his business system to the franchises with customer satisfaction at the heart of a strategy to make Ontario Auto Collision CARSTAR as familiar to consumers as Speedy mufflers and Harvey's hamburgers.

"We're trying to elevate the body shop industry to higher standards, says Mercanti, whose company is highly ranked by the Coyote Vision Group which represents the North American industry.

The emphasis on customer satisfaction includes the provision of five-year warranties, honoured at all Ontario Auto Collisions CARSTAR and CARSTAR locations in Canada.

It's all part of a company-wide effort to go the extra mile for its customers.

"We want to do more than just satisfy the customer," Mercanti stresses.

"We want to delight them."

▶

*Sam Mercanti is the founding CEO of both Ontario Auto Collision CARSTAR and CARSTAR Automotive Canada.*
– PHOTO BY DAVID GRUGGEN

# CarStar Automotive

*Success* 103 *Stories*

# London Telecom

That long distance feeling was causing Rob Freeman some acute financial discomfort.

In the late 1980s, Freeman was a Southwestern Ontario real estate broker who regularly made long distance calls between his Strathroy office and London.

"I was spending between $100 to $150 a month – a fortune in long-distance calls," recalls Freeman who is today sole owner, chairman and CEO of London Telecom Network.

"As part of my real estate business, I had to make regular calls to Strathroy," he adds, recalling cost concerns caused him to reduce the duration of calls to clients, a move which only hurt his business.

There seemed little he could do. It was two years, he explains, before the CRTC allowed anyone to resell long distance telephone services. Bell Canada still held a monopoly on long distance calls – and they were expensive.

Eager to find some way to reduce his long distance bill without cutting back on telephone calls, Freeman turned his attention to Mount Brydges, a small community midway between London and Strathroy – and well within local calling range to either larger centre.

Freeman wondered if it might be possible to "put in some kind of switching box," in Mount Brydges so that all his calls between London and Strathroy could be bounced through Mount Brydges to make these calls 'local' and therefore free of long distance charges.

Freeman discovered that the CRTC legislation of the day didn't even anticipate – let alone forbid – such a move so he took out a $10,000 small ventures loan and established a call divert system with 10 lines in the basement of a friend's Mount Brydges home.

With his "one-hop" system in place, Freeman was now in the telecommunications business. Not only would he save money by his turning long distance calls into local calls, he would also collect money from anyone wanting to access his system for savings of their own.

Freeman called his new business CSM (Call Share Management) and signed up 400 customers interested in making calls between London and Strathroy for a flat fee of $15 a month.

And Freeman saw in all of this, an even bigger business opportunity.

With his car serving as a mobile office, Freeman headed east to Burlington in 1990 where he set up a call divert system in Oakville, making Toronto a local call for his Burlington clients.

He then moved his head office to the basement of a Victorian home at Guelph Line and Harvester Road in Burlington.

Freeman became the subject of an influential Hamilton Spectator article which prompted 1,200 more people to subscribe over the next few months.

> "We were the right company at the right time. Demand kept growing as more and more consumers opted for lower phone bills."

The CRTC ordered deregulation of the telephone industry in 1992, permitting greater competition, allowing Freeman to lease band width from Bell to join the Hamilton area to Toronto as London Telecom's newest service area.

In 1993, Freeman renamed his firm London Telecom Inc. and left real estate to concentrate full-time on telecommunications. His clientele grew rapidly in Hamilton and beyond.

Buoyed by this response, Freeman moved London Telecom headquarters to Hamilton in 1994, initially across the street from The Spectator, then into a more spacious 9,000-square-foot location down the street from the venerable Frid Street newspaper.

Robert Belliveau, vice-president of marketing and regulatory matters, joined London Telecom in 1993 and remembers well the sense of excitement surrounding the fast-growing company.

"We were definitely the right company at the right time," recalls Belliveau. "The demand kept growing as more and more consumers opted for lower phone bills."

"The CRTC has been very successful in driving down rates," Belliveau adds. "Consumers pay half of what they paid prior to deregulation – and London Telecom customers pay even less, perhaps a third of what they paid in 1992."

London Telecom offers several attractive packages. For residential customers, five hours of long distance calling is yours for just $29.95 plus tax per month. Ten hours are available for $49.95 and 40 hours for $74.95. Add $20 and you can also make calls to the U.S.

Commercial rates are $10 more for 5-10 hours and $20 more for 40 hours.

"We appeal equally to residential and commercial clients," says Belliveau.

To access the system, you simply set your phone to automatically speed dial your 7-digit access number, then you dial the area code and phone number.

By 1993, London Telecom had linked together several networks across Southern Ontario offering 40 hours of calling within the network at a flat rate of less than 4 cents a minute, a rate that continues today.

And, by the mid-1990s, London Telecom Network was a multi-million-dollar enterprise encompassing every major city in Ontario and Quebec.

Today, the network extends across nine of Canada's 10 provinces, excluding only Saskatchewan for regulatory reasons.

Accolades continued pouring in: London Telecom won the 1994 Hamilton and District Chamber of Commerce Business Achievement Award and the 1994 Ontario Chamber of Commerce Award of Merit. Ontario Business Journal cited the company year after year as one of the province's top 10 entrepreneurs and London Telecom won a Gold ACE (Awarding Creative Excellence) Award from the Hamilton Ad and Sales Club.

Beyond the low, flat rate charge for long distance calls, London Telecom's most popular feature is its Reverse Calling service allowing the friends and family of customers to call the customer and reverse the charge at no added cost to either party. The duration of the call is simply calculated into the customer's allowable limit.

▶

*Rob Freeman connected with a good idea in the late 1980s and he has been making the right calls ever since.*
*– PHOTO BY DAVID GRUGGEN*

## London Telecom

*Success* 105 *Stories*

# London Telecom

In 1996, the London Telecom Network headquarters relocated to 30,000 square feet of space on the sixth and seventh floors of the Oakville Corporate Centre off Dorval Drive and the QEW.

However, the headquarters of the parent company, The London Telecom Group Inc., remains in London, not far from Freeman's home in the nearby community of Lambeth. Here, he's a assisted by Chief Operating Officer Jim Weisz and Chief Financial Officer Colin Wood.

London Telecom Group is today the head office and holding company for about a dozen subsidiaries, including London Telecom Network Inc., one of Canada's oldest alternative long distance service providers of voice and data telecommunications products and services to clients across North America.

Reselling services in the United States are provided by a sister subsidiary, London Telecom Network Corp. of Minneapolis, Minnesota.

Other major subsidiaries include London Telecom Data Services Inc., providing protection of electronic information; and LTN Communications Centre Inc., telecommunication products retail outlets in London and Huntsville with additional outlets on the way.

And, there's also Vancouver-based WinTel Communications Inc., London Telecom's equal-access, per minute, long distance service allowing customers to call anywhere in Canada and the United States (except Alaska and Hawaii) for just 13 cents per minute.

London Telecom itself also services much of the North American market using a combination of owned and leased fibre optic band width transmission facilities and equipment.

Driving the company's success is its ability to offer significant savings.

"London Telecom provides the consumer the predictability of knowing what their long distance phone bill will be each month so they can budget accordingly," says Robert Belliveau.

"We offer predictability, stability, affordability – and, above all, peace of mind," adds the marketing vice-president.

Today, the London Telecom Group employs over 200 people and nearly doubles its revenue base each year.

Freeman believes his debt-free, private company's growth rate is sustainable. But, he's determined to take a measured approach for continued growth.

"Slow and steady is my personal motto," says Freeman.

"I'm in this for the long term."

*Success Stories*

# London Telecom

▲ The London Telecom Network has its headquarters in the Oakville Corporate Centre.

– PHOTO BY DAVID GRUGGEN

# CHAPTER 8
# On The Homefront

# On The Homefront

Shelter. Next to food and sleep, it's perhaps our most basic human need. It's not surprising, therefore, that fulfilling this fundamental need has given rise to an enormous housing-related industry. And one of the most vibrant real estate markets in Canada is, well, housed in our own vast economic region.

Compare the housing prices and values found in the sprawling economic region from Niagara Falls-to-Oakville and it quickly becomes apparent that the Hamilton-Wentworth, Niagara and Halton regions offer astonishing real estate bargains, unmatched in other metropolitan centres such as Toronto, Vancouver or Montreal.

A home remains one of the most popular means of building an investment – while the owner receives the enjoyment of living in it as well. And, a home remains the largest single investment most people will ever make in their entire lifetime.

The demand for our economic region's high-quality, affordable homes has given rise to a vibrant housing industry which includes everything from new and resale homes to related services such as renovations and expansion projects or restorations of homes after fire or water damage.

Residential construction industry concerns are regularly championed by the Hamilton-Halton Home Builders' Association, while commercial, institutional and industrial construction is the domain of the Hamilton Construction Association.

Founded in 1920, the HCA brings together general contractors, trade contractors, suppliers, manufacturers and other construction related interests into a single organization providing a united voice for the construction industry. With more than 400 members, the HCA is the "voice of construction" for Hamilton-Wentworth, Halton and Haldimand-Norfolk regions and Brant County.

The HHHBA and HCA are among the associations providing an organized approach to serving an enormous housing and related services market. How vibrant this market is during any given year depends in large part on intangible elements such as consumer confidence and job security.

"Ultimately, housing sales and housing starts are tied to the health of the manufacturing sector," says Neil Everson, manager of business development for Hamilton-Wentworth Economic Development Department. "Whether or not you buy a home depends in large measure on how well industry is doing."

> "Ultimately, housing sales and housing starts are tied to the health of the manufacturing sector."

"If industry is doing well, the service sector is also likely doing well, and this translates into increased job security and employment growth," Everson adds. These are the things you need to stimulate the housing market. People won't buy if they're afraid of losing their jobs."

Low interest rates, affordable prices and a wide selection have boosted consumer confidence. As a result, new home construction is enjoying significant growth throughout the Hamilton Census Metropolitan Area, according to statistics released by CMHC (Canada Mortgage and Housing Corporation).

CMHC reports a total of 2,642 homes were built in 1996 in the Hamilton CMA taking in Hamilton-Wentworth, Burlington and Grimsby. That's a 29 per cent increase over 2,001 homes in 1995.

By the fall of 1997, a total of 2,423 housing starts were under way in the Hamilton CMA, compared to just 1,710 starts in the first eight months of 1995.

In the month of August 1997 alone, single-family, fully detached housing starts increased 55 per cent to 242 units from 156 units in August 1996 in the Hamilton CMA. Builders were reporting difficulties in keeping up with demand as consumer confidence brought a surge of new home buyers into the market.

For the St. Catharines-Niagara CMA, CMHC reports 995 housing starts in 1996, compared to just 898 starts in this metropolitan area taking in most of Niagara region.

In 1996, realtors experienced one of their strongest years ever across the Metropolitan Hamilton area encompassing the Hamilton-Wentworth region, Burlington, Grimsby and other neighbouring communities.

This area's resale housing market has also been experiencing strong sales.

Buoyed by one of the strongest December sales months in recent years, 1996 sales were up 31 per cent over 1995, according to MLS (Multiple Listing Service) statistics released by the Metropolitan Hamilton Real Estate Board.

While average house prices remained fairly stable, sales increased to 10,784 units for 1996, compared with 8,185 resales in 1995, a gain 1996 Board President Bob Schinkel attributed to low mortgage rates and affordable house prices.

This healthy trend was alive and well during the first eight months of 1997 when 7,547 resale homes changed hands, up 4 per cent from 7,200 sales in the first eight months of 1996.

Perhaps even more noteworthy was a full 7 per cent increase in average prices, taking the sale price of an average home in Metro Hamilton to $152,524 compared with $142,498 a year earlier.

By the fall of 1997, the average two-storey home in Ancaster had a selling price of $257,000, up 4 per cent from the selling price of $245,586 in 1996.

In Burlington, two-storey homes gained 12 per cent to sell for almost $258,000 while Hamilton Mountain's average two-storey home increased in price 4 per cent to $170,112.

Marie Kachmarsky, 1997 board president, cites several factors for continuing growth in sales and selling prices.

"With a good supply of houses available in a wide range of prices and affordable mortgage rates," says Kachmarsky, "it's a great time to buy."

# On The Homefront

*An aerial view of the Strawberry Hill subdivision, one of several major developments in the Hamilton area in the last decade. Consisting of single-family homes and located in Hamilton's east end, it was a project of George Sinclair Construction.*

Kachmarsky's comments are echoed by Bud Sinclair, president of George Sinclair Construction, who is following a rich family tradition of building attractive, affordable homes.

And you certainly won't find Chris Medcalf arguing against any assertion that it's a great time to buy. Medcalf is also part of a generational family business active in the housing industry.

Like Sinclair Construction, the Medcalf and Associates realty firm places an emphasis on service and customer care.

Further helping to serve the housing market are other related industries such as the renovations firm Birchside Builders and damage-restorers Paul's Restorations.

These companies can also be found in this book's directory. We'll take a closer look at Sinclair, Medcalf, Birchside and Paul's in a series of profiles, next.

*Success Stories*

# George Sinclair Construction

The Sinclairs' rise to developer prominence is built on a cornerstone they fashioned more than half a century ago.

In the early 1940s, Sinclair Cut Stone laid the foundation for many prominent government and institutional buildings in Ontario. It was then that the company founder George Sinclair began building his family's own road to success, a road that would be extended and redefined by generations of Sinclairs.

After serving with the Royal Canadian Air Force, entrepreneurial son Bill Sinclair returned to his parents' Cameron Avenue, Hamilton home with his wife Margit. There, he had worked in the cut stone business, as well as made and sold model airplane kits.

In 1949, Bill Sinclair and his father George decided to move on.

George Sinclair Construction Ltd. began building homes on Holmesdale Avenue near Parkdale.

Then, after buying 26 lots at Pottruff and King Street East, the Sinclairs built the Orkney Park subdivision, named for Scotland's Orkney Islands, birthplace of the Sinclair ancestral clan.

They prided themselves on building the entire house, right down to the kitchen cabinets, stairs and window frames, all fashioned by craftsmen in a workshop converted from an old barn.

In 1952, the Sinclairs built a dozen homes at Beland Court. With son Bud due to be born, Bill Sinclair took one of the ranch-style bungalows for himself and lived there the rest of his life.

Through the 1950s, the Sinclairs continued building homes in Hamilton's east end. Houses sold for $11,000 to $20,000 in an age when suits – with two sets of pants – were yours for $60.

In the 1960s, the Sinclairs studied an ancient Roman housing concept known as condominiums – and they built the area's first condominium complex, at Lake Avenue and Barton Street.

By the time George Sinclair died in 1967, Bill Sinclair was aggressively pursuing developments in new lands.

Bill Sinclair opened up much of Hamilton's far east end for development, insisting on the realignment of Barton Street East and the filling of some wetlands to bring housing into new areas. He was also responsible for the reservoir that made development possible at Dewitt Road in Stoney Creek.

Teaming up with developer Charlie Campbell, the pair started up Queenston Developments which was responsible for the development of the area between Nash Road and Centennial Parkway and between Queenston Road and the Niagara Escarpment that proved key to opening up the east region to growth.

Bill Sinclair's pioneering development role was often challenged by those who opposed change. "My dad was known for his determination to build in areas that

> "We live by that adage, to try and put more in than we take out. Let's face it, these are the people who put us where we are today."

some people wanted him out of," recalls son Bud Sinclair, who had watched some of the clashes unfold as a teenager working part-time for the family company, cutting lawns at model homes.

"My dad couldn't accept people saying no for the sake of saying no," recollects Bud Sinclair, who is today the company's president. "He always tried to make development happen in a way everyone could live with," he explains.

Bud Sinclair remembers the furor over his father's determination to build Lakewood Landing, a collection of homes at Grays Road and the Lake Ontario shoreline in Stoney Creek.

"Some people just assumed that building houses anywhere near there would wipe out a population of turtles," he says. "In fact, the turtles that were to be protected didn't even live there and the ones that did live there didn't mind a bit. The turtle became dad's unofficial mascot."

Bud Sinclair recalls another clash with environmentalists when Bill Sinclair spearheaded the Dewitt Heights subdivision on the Niagara Bench, a plateau part-way up the Niagara Escarpment.

"My dad won that battle and today it's one of the nicest housing areas you'll find anywhere. It was a gravel pit before he owned it. But he preserved many of the trees and kept its natural appeal. He got his point across that housing can exist in harmony with nature."

In addition to building some of the best-built homes in the area, Bill Sinclair contributed heavily to community causes and served as president of Hamilton East Kiwanis Club.

When asked about his devotion to the community, Bill Sinclair said: "We live by that adage, to try and put more in than we take out. Let's face it, these are the people who put us where we are today."

All told, the Sinclairs built over 2,100 housing units in more than half a century of business. Other developments include a Caledonia subdivision, the Summerfield subdivision on Hamilton's West Mountain, the 100-acre Wellington Chase subdivision on Hamilton's Central Mountain and Strawberry Hill near Stoney Creek.

As a past president of the Hamilton and District Home Builders' Association, and past director of the Ontario Council, Bill Sinclair participated in all levels of the home builders' association in the effort to protect the industry from government intervention, expensive levies and unnecessary taxes and to provide economical inexpensive housing for the new home buyer.

Bill Sinclair's determination to develop new land, perseverance in overcoming obstacles, dedication to the home building industry, integrity, community support, and his ability to strike a balance between needed development and the environment, did not go unnoticed.

In 1979, Bill Sinclair received the HDHBA's Distinguished Service Award.

In the 1980s he twice won the Paul Wright Memorial Award for industry excellence. And in 1990, the HDHBA inducted Bill Sinclair into their builders' Hall of Fame.

Bill Sinclair died of a heart attack, in 1996, at the age of 76.

▶

*Bud Sinclair continues to build on a rich family tradition dating back to 1949.*
– PHOTO BY DAVID GRUGGEN

# George Sinclair Construction

*Success* 113 *Stories*

# George Sinclair Construction

*George Sinclair Construction has been one of the region's best-known builders for over 50 years. Sinclair's Strawberry Hill subdivision, completed in the 1980s, is among the builder's many successes.*
– PHOTO BY DAVID GRUGGEN

*Some of Sinclair's first homes in the city were built on Holmesdale Ave. in 1949. Today, Sinclair continues to build many fine homes. A recent project, in Grimsby, is shown at the beginning of this chapter.*

*Success Stories*

# George Sinclair Construction

*Bud Sinclair shares a special moment with his father Bill as the two reminisce about the man who started it all – family patriarch George Sinclair. Today, Bud is president of Sinclair Construction, taking the helm after his father's death in 1996.*
*– PHOTO BY BOB CHAMBERS*

**B**ill Sinclair's family was always an important part of his business.

His daughters Elaine and Shirley along with son Bud all participated in the business as well as friends and other relatives.

"You didn't just work for Bill Sinclair; you became a part of his family," says Mary Estok, Bill's longtime office manager and friend for over 40 years. This type of personal dedication made Sinclair Construction truly a "Family Business."

Today, Bud Sinclair, who has won several awards of his own, carries on a family tradition of excellence and has pinned future success on the company's ability to best serve its niche market.

"It's not just a plan on paper, this is something we put our heart into," explains Bud Sinclair, who would like to see the company continue on in the same spirit into the 21st century.

"We're building someone's home in a real community with its own personality," he says. "When my dad and I would drive past some of the homes he built, I still remember how proud he was to think he was responsible for contributing to the growth of his community and the families who would live there."

"We've never wanted to be one of the biggest builders. Just one of the best."

*Success Stories*

# Birchside Builders Inc.

If you can dream it – we can build it. This is no mere advertising boast.

For Birchside Builders, the imaginative slogan is closer to a simple statement of fact, a self-imposed challenge to turn every customer's vision into reality.

"Nothing is more satisfying than to have a customer who is very pleased with your hard work," asserts Wes Votruba, president of the Ancaster-based building renovations firm.

That feeling of satisfaction is becoming quite familiar to Votruba whose company has improved the homes of steelworkers, university professors, lawyers, doctors, retirees and prominent citizens.

Votruba is now contemplating a move into building entire homes. It's an understandable move, given that his 20-year-old firm has already built a few additions that are larger than some homes.

One of the more memorable Birchside projects is a striking, stone, two-storey addition to a Westdale home.

Another Birchside project features a spacious den boasting wooden-beamed cathedral ceilings, oak floors, French doors and a cozy fireplace.

"We can provide an addition to an older home that will blend in so well, you can't tell it's an addition," Votruba says with pride, crediting his employees for superb custom-made additions.

Votruba's most impressive project remains his palatial Old Dundas Road, Ancaster office-home.

After tackling some major renovation and addition jobs, Votruba built – and later renovated – his three-storey, five-bedroom, 6,000-square-foot home with indoor swimming pool.

With its panoramic view of Hamilton's distant skyline, Votruba's office-home is a world away from his youthful life as an escapee from communist Czechoslovakia.

The stifling Communist influence proved intolerable for Votruba, who was born and raised in the town of As in Czechoslovakia (now Czech Republic), near the former border dividing East and West Germany.

"I was 17 years old when my parents put me on a plane for Canada," he recalls, noting his 1969 escape came just a year after the Russians invaded the country to clamp down on liberal reforms introduced during the Prague Spring of 1968.

"My parents didn't want me to live under a communist regime so they sent me to a land of opportunity," he adds.

"It was an adventure."

Following his escape, Votruba moved in with relatives while his mother, father and sisters all remained in the former Czechoslovakia under the surveillance of the secret police.

The government punished his sister, he explains, by preventing the would-be nurse from furthering her education. She eventually received her nursing degree after resorting to night classes.

> *My dream was to run my own business. Since my interests leaned towards carpentry, that's what I went into.*

"They had already punished my parents," says Votruba, explaining that just before he was born, his father, Vaclav, a degree holding engineer, was sent to the salt mines and restricted to labour work following a failed escape attempt.

Although he spoke little English, the young Votruba brought to his adopted homeland the work ethic of his father and business sense of his grandfather, also named Vaclav. "They were both major influences," recalls Votruba.

"My grandfather had his own butcher shop business and several houses that were confiscated and then returned to him. He worked hard, he never complained, he earned his success."

Just a year after arriving in Canada, an 18-year-old Votruba moved out on his own and took a job in a now-defunct cotton mill in Hamilton.

He was promoted to foreman even though he spoke little English, a problem he rectified through night classes. "One morning I woke up and I was thinking in English. That's when I really began to think of myself as being Canadian."

Jobs in steel mills and a gas bar followed but Votruba remained restless. "My dream was to run my own business," he says. "To achieve that, I felt I needed a trade and since my interests leaned towards carpentry, that's what I went into."

Votruba teamed up with friend Otto Boril to form B&V Construction in the early 1970s to perform household renovations and repairs.

After Boril left the business in the mid-1970s, Votruba married, and he and his wife Sandy continued running B&V for several years. They changed the name of their business to Birch Construction before settling on Birchside Builders Inc., a firm which has long emphasized its high-quality workmanship.

"The name comes from Birch wood and it puts us near the top of any alphabetical list of renovators," says Sandy Votruba, who juggles family life and company bookkeeping and computer work from the home her husband designed and built in 1989.

With a core staff of five plus sub-contractors, the consistently profitable, long-established company tackles 40-50 renovation projects a year, ranging in value from $5,000 to $250,000.

Blueprints and estimates are rapidly produced via computer programs designed by Votruba to enable his small company to respond quickly to customer needs.

"We always have to be willing to change," notes Votruba, "to try new ways of doing things – to make sure we're always one step ahead of the competition."

Determined to grow his business gradually and perhaps one day branch out into whole home construction, Votruba clearly finds his work to be a strong source of satisfaction.

"I enjoy custom jobs, I enjoy working with people and solving any problems in a friendly way," says Votruba, who continues to build his business on referrals.

"We bring a lot of creativity to our renovation solutions. Our satisfaction comes from taking our customers' ideas and building an addition that's everything they'd dreamed of."

▶

*Wes Votruba stands in front of the home he built for his family. The house is an example of the workmanship provided by Votruba and Birchside Builders Inc.*
*– PHOTO BY DAVID GRUGGEN*

# Birchside Builders Inc.

Success  117  Stories

# Medcalf & Associates Limited

Cheer up – call Medcalf, was a familiar slogan Roman Jankevicius didn't want to hear.

The Hamilton man was attempting, unsuccessfully, to sell his Carrick Avenue home privately. Now he had realtor Chris Medcalf in his living room, boldly stating he could sell the house, quickly, no problem. Annoyed, he called Medcalf's bluff.

The house sold, quickly, no problem.

Buoyed by this fast mid-1980s sale, Jankevicius went on to list and sell several other houses through Medcalf and Associates Ltd.

This challenge solved, Medcalf turned his attention to another matter of interest: rival real estate agent Donna Bacher, who often competed for east end listings.

Medcalf found an unusual way to take out the competition: He married her. Best man at the wedding: Roman Jankevicius.

"I'm sure it was a plot," Donna Medcalf recalls with mock indignation. "I got busy taking care of our kids and Chris got busy taking care of my clients."

The ability of Chris Medcalf, 36, to win people over may be partly genetic in origin. His father, Harvey Medcalf, established the family's real estate roots half a century ago when he returned to Hamilton from Second World War service.

And it was Harvey Medcalf who first made use of the Medcalf "cheer up" phrase. "I was in the habit of saying it – and I must have used that phrase a lot, because people started calling me Cheer Up," recollects Harvey Medcalf, 79.

'Cheer Up Medcalf' spent 1947-1949 with J. Harold Foley Real Estate – a pivotal period in local realty history. It was during this time that Harvey Medcalf and others in the real estate industry decided to create a co-operative system for listing each others properties for sale.

Although it initially involved just half-a-dozen realty firms, this new system would evolve into the MLS or Multiple Listing Service which is today the bread and butter of all real estate sales people in the Greater Hamilton area and beyond.

Simply put, the MLS lists properties for sale by real estate professionals, a tremendous benefit for sales people who can use the listings to build their business and offer prospective home buyers a wide choice of resale housing stock.

"Up until we came up with the new system, the real estate people just ignored each other," Harvey Medcalf recalls in an interview at the company's King Street East at Cameron Street office. "This system really helped people find the right house. It was a step in the right direction."

Having helped make realty history, he went into business on his own in 1949.

As Harvey Medcalf began building up his business, his "Cheer Up" slogan began appearing on everything from stationary and business cards to coffee cups, mugs, even company cheques inviting the recipient to "cheer up to the sum of . . ."

Did the "Cheer Up – Call Medcalf" slogan have the psychological effect of

> "All that matters is you and your client. You don't need a big name, big numbers or a big network behind you."

making people feel better about selling or buying, thereby increasing sales? Harvey Medcalf shrugs. "Psychological effect? I *do* know that it's made us a lot of money."

Recently retired after nearly half a century in business and many thousands of sales, Harvey Medcalf is almost 80. But he still turns up daily at the Medcalf office, a homey bungalow once converted into doctors examining rooms – before being converted again into realty offices.

"Real estate is my life – I can't get enough of it. I still like to see how sales are progressing and what's being sold."

And Harvey Medcalf likes what he sees. "Chris is a real go-getter, a great salesman who makes a lot of sales. I gave him an established company name – but he's made the sales happen on his own. He's very successful."

A father praising a son. For a less-biased assessment I spoke with a former competitor. "Chris would be outstanding no matter who he worked for," says Donna Medcalf (well, she is a former rival). "He's very service-oriented, hardworking and great at making sales."

Of course, the numbers speak for themselves. Chris Medcalf routinely makes 120 sales per year, 100 sales in a slow year, extremely high numbers for an individual making sales without a support staff.

Key to his success is an established approach, honed since he entered the business in 1980 at the age of 19: Focus on the customer's needs, work hard and be as good as your word.

"All that matters is you and your client," asserts Chris Medcalf. "You don't need to have a big name, big numbers or a big network behind you."

"There's certainly a place for the big companies," he explains, "but there's also a niche for us as well. A lot of people like our homey atmosphere. They like dealing with a smaller company."

Medcalf and Associates employs no more than a dozen people, all of them carefully screened to ensure they live up to the company's reputation for straightforward, honest service.

"And if we make a mistake, we'll make it right," states Chris Medcalf, who has served on arbitration and professional standards committees of the Metropolitan Hamilton Real Estate Board.

"We care about the families we serve, we get to know them and we grow through repeat business," adds Medcalf, who has handled real estate transactions for clients whose parents bought a home from his father.

Strict attention to service has helped make Medcalf a strong independent office, a 50-year success story with a promising future and a history of supporting community causes and youth sports teams, including the teams of Medcalf children, Harvey, Melissa and Zachary.

Certainly, no one needs to tell Chris Medcalf to cheer up.

"Whenever any of us have a bad day, we say that we're glad that day is over – and we can't wait for tomorrow," he says with a grin. "I love my job. Every day is a new opportunity."

▶

*Chris Medcalf, with his father Harvey, the man behind the company's well-known 'Cheer Up – Call Medcalf' slogan.*
*– PHOTO BY DAVID GRUGGEN*

# Medcalf & Associates Limited

Success 119 Stories

# Paul's Restorations

There's no such thing as a routine day at Paul's Restorations.

"We never know what the next hour will bring, let alone the whole day," admits Paul Giardini, president of the Hamilton-based disaster repair, cleaning and restorations company.

"Storms, fires, tornadoes, all come up suddenly – you can't plan for anything," adds Giardini, 45, who frequently works evenings and weekends responding to insurance claim work.

And, Giardini doesn't hesitate to roll up his own sleeves to personally sweep up glass or mop floors at a disaster site.

"It's honest work," he shrugs, "and it's got us where we are today."

Paul's Restorations prides itself on responding quickly to an emergency, often assembling a cleaning team to meet the needs of insurance companies, adjusters and homeowners. Paul's serves leading insurance companies including Halifax, Zurich, Dominion of Canada, The Co-Operators, The Royal and Gore Mutual.

Paul's services everything from flooded basements and wind-torn shingles to major fires at office complexes.

"We won't become complacent," says Giardini. "We respond immediately – and we can usually prepare an estimate the same day," he adds. "We work closely with adjusters. Service, service, service is the name of the game."

This dedicated approach has won Paul's Restorations a growing share of the insurance claims business. From $100,000 in 1982, its first year of business, revenue grew to $10 million by 1997.

Through all its years of growth, Paul's has never forgotten the lessons learned throughout Giardini's life in Hamilton.

Born in Italy, Paul Giardini arrived in Hamilton at age four. He grew up in the city's east end; an unpretentious, working class community where he developed a determined approach to achieving success.

Giardini was barely out of high school when he began to work in the construction business. As an employee he proved devoted to his work, earning recognition as an employee of the month and as one firm's youngest-ever superintendent.

While working full-time hours during eight years with Stelco's engineering services, he began a part-time, home-based business known as Paul's Restorations and Contracting. "Then a friend of mine suggested I get into the insurance restoration business," Giardini recollects.

"I began to discover a market and a need for this work," he explains. "Before long, I was sitting across my banker's desk with a business plan in hand. I remember feeling excited and scared."

By 1982, the company had grown into a full-time concern and was renamed Paul's Restorations. It began to handle small claims work such as vandalism, kitchen fires and break-ins.

> "We won't become complacent. We respond immediately... service, service, service is the name of the game."

A more focused Paul's Restorations started marketing itself to agents and insurance companies and steadily the PR logo gained recognition and trust in the industry. The business soon outgrew its home-based location and two succeeding commercial locations.

Then, in 1990, it moved to its current location, a modern 12,500-square-foot, office and warehouse facility on Upper Ottawa Street, south of Rymal Road.

By this point, Giardini finally allowed himself the luxury of a regular paycheque. Previously, he had re-invested the earnings into the business. The family expenses were covered by his supportive wife Rita, a Hamilton school teacher.

Paul's Restorations continued to respond to the needs of the industry and grew into a multi-service company which could take care of emergency services, building restoration, content restoration, consulting and warehousing.

The firm became relied upon by insurance companies desiring restoration firms capable of handling all claims, big and small, from start to finish.

Giardini continues to invest in the business. To provide a one-stop shop for insurance companies and insureds, the firm opened up Jonathon's Floorings, which restores, cleans and replaces tile, carpet and other floor surfaces. It's also opened Manor Cleaners, which promptly serves insureds whose clothing and draperies are damaged by smoke or water.

In 1994, Paul's formed a partnership with Allen and Philip Fracassi, the entrepreneurial brothers who have achieved enormous success with Philip Services.

Their goal was to expand the business further and open new licensed locations.

This goal was achieved later that same year with the opening of the first licensed Paul's location, in Oakville.

By 1997, Paul's had expanded into Aurora, Barrie, Brantford, Mississauga and Waterloo, bringing the total to seven locations. At Hamilton head office alone, there are about 40 people, including seven estimator/job contractors and 14 cleaning and support staff.

All told there are over 70 people employed at the various Paul's locations, plus an array of equipment and a total fleet of 30 service vehicles, allowing the company to draw on a pool of talent from across Southern Ontario.

Paul's can quickly assemble disaster teams with enough professionals and equipment to perform jobs of any size.

From his first major claim – a badly burned-out, two-storey building – Giardini now looks back on a satisfying career based on the conscientious provision of professional disaster repair and cleaning services. And it's a career which shows no signs of slowing down. Company outlets and overall clientele continue to grow.

Driving the company's success is a clear understanding, by every member of Paul's team, that their work can be of significant benefit to people whose homes have been damaged by fire, wind or water.

"Our professional teams realize that we restore and clean more than buildings and contents," says Giardini.

"We restore homes and places of work and we clean prized possessions. We are all dedicated to servicing the needs of troubled insureds – not just the claims."

▶
*Paul Giardini has transformed a small business started in 1982 into a company which today employs over 70 people.*
*– PHOTO BY DAVID GRUGGEN*

Success Stories

# Paul's Restorations

*Success* 121 *Stories*

– PHOTO BY DAVID GRUGGEN

# CHAPTER 9

# *A Look Ahead*

# A Look Ahead

Our vast, regional economy will continue to diversify in the coming years, with high-technology companies playing a larger role as an employer and net contributor to the area's wealth. The nature of work will also continue to change through an accelerated evolution which will move even further away from the traditional employer concept to a model favouring contract agents, rather than employees, working from virtual offices, rather than buildings.

"People still need a sense of belonging and camaraderie," notes Lee Kirkby, the former executive director of the Hamilton and District Chamber of Commerce.

"But rather than a traditional staff arrangement, we'll probably see associations and associate groups of people coming together in a virtual corporation to put out a particular project," Kirkby suggests. "In fact, this would be even less defined than a virtual corporation, although it would act like one."

"While the group is working together they may appear to be much like any staff of people anywhere," he adds, "or they may be scattered all over the country, working out of their homes, linked together by computers and phone lines."

"But when the project is completed, the group disbands until the next project when a different group may then come together, perhaps with some of the same members and some new members," Kirkby says.

"The key to all of this," he adds, "is that they bring with them the specific skills sets needed to take on the new project and bring it to a successful completion."

Kirkby suggests that a successful variation of this model can be found in many real estate offices which consist of a series of cubicles rented by individual sales people who perform independently but in association with the real estate brokerage which provides office space, computers, telephones and other commercial infrastructure for a fee.

"Although there can be less security and stability with this approach, it also gives individuals the freedom they need to pursue their own goals," notes Kirkby.

Success in the new millennium will depend in large part on an ability to adapt quickly to rapidly changing new technology.

Kirkby asserts that successful individuals and companies will be those embracing new technology, mastering it and wringing from it every meaningful benefit it can offer.

"When I first became executive director of the chamber in the late 1980s, we were using the services of an offset printer to produce all our documents," he recalls. "Now we produce our own documents using a photocopier, with high-quality results, thanks to advances in technology which have enabled us to expand our capabilities."

"Flexibility to adapt to changing technology is absolutely crucial to business success," adds Kirkby, who left the chamber in 1997 to become manager of the document imaging department at Leppert's Office Equipment.

In his new role, Kirkby is heavily involved in conducting much of the consulting and independent sales work he refers to. He's now directly involved in assisting business people in making a technological leap into high-tech equipment which can perform work regarding indexing systems and other data processing functions in a fraction of the time. "The return on investment in using this new equipment is so high and so fast, it actually pays people to invest in the system," he says.

This emphasis on high technology bodes well for some of our economic region's high-tech leaders, including Wescam Inc., a manufacturer and supplier of gyro-stabilized camera mount equipment used in everything from Hollywood blockbuster movies to the Olympics and other major events to military and police surveillance work.

Other examples of local high-tech firms include Gennum Inc., a manufacturer of circuitry and hearing instrument components; Zenon, makers of membrane-based water filtration systems; BCL Magnetics; Dynamic and Proto Circuits; Antel Optronics, a fibre optic wire producer; and CRS Robotics, manufacturers of industrial robots adept at performing the dull, dangerous and dirty jobs unsuited to human beings. All of these high-tech leaders are serving niche markets for highly specialized technology. These markets appear to constantly evolve rapidly and mutate into a myriad of newly created opportunities.

For those capable companies willing to change and grow with this fast-evolving technology, the future appears bright indeed.

And the computer revolution is shifting into high gear.

In Ontario, nearly one in every three adults has access to, and makes use of, a computer every week. The usage is growing across Canada and the number of household personal computers is also on the rise.

Yet as we've seen throughout this book, success isn't confined to those who embrace the latest technology.

Traditional, industrial companies such as Dominion Pattern Works have been able to survive and thrive in downsized markets. Major steelmakers such as Stelco and Dofasco have adopted numerous technological improvements and, in many ways, have evolved into what can be considered high-tech entities.

Past predictions that high-tech industries would replace whole sectors have largely proven false. What we've seen instead is the shrinkage of some sectors, but by no means their replacement.

Traditional heavy manufacturing has survived. Steelmakers, though downsized, remain major employers.

There is no widening chasm between high-tech firms and other manufacturers as virtually all firms have adopted some forms of high technology. There is instead a blurring of definitions regarding a given company's qualifications for "high-tech" status.

# A Look Ahead

The fatal flaw running through many dire predictions of a "post-industrial" future is the assumption that traditional industries would remain static, fail to evolve and collapse like dinosaurs from their own cumbersome weight.

In fact, many traditional industries have evolved, assumed some high-tech characteristics, and continued production more efficiently and effectively than ever.

Another major flaw inherent in some widely bandied-about forecasts is the erroneous belief that Canada and other modern Western nations would lose their basic industries to developing nations. Whole societies were to just quietly sit back and watch a major part of our economies, a major source of jobs and prosperity, simply disappear.

Quite frankly, I've always found the notion, that we'll stop making steel and instead buy it from the Third World, a little hard to accept, especially when you consider the high technology – and high quality – inherent in thin gauge, high-strength automotive steel products. Believe it or not, not every country makes these products as well as we do. Canadian-made steel is here to stay.

Equally suspect are the tired predictions I heard throughout the 1980s and 1990s while I was employed as a journalist with The Hamilton Spectator. Television and computers were to replace newspapers. Rather than spend a dollar on a newspaper, dads were to spend thousands of dollars on computer systems and then monopolize the TV to watch words scroll down a screen. Instead, what should have been a predictable trend emerged.

Newspapers across the country experienced circulation shrinkage but only a few have actually disappeared.

Some papers, The Spectator included, discovered the secret to recapturing readers lay not in emulating television with short items and lots of pictures.

The secret lay in offering readers what the electronic media has difficulty offering: Lengthy, in-depth stories and analysis that can be read and re-read at leisure. After years of decline, The Spectator's circulation is again growing.

Once again, we found simplistic warnings of one medium or industry replacing another were unfounded. The vast consumer market simply found room for more TV and radio stations and a reduced number of newspapers. The Toronto Telegram's death did not signal the beginning of the end of newspapers. It marked, instead, the beginning of the Toronto Sun and the Sun Syndicate.

And, there are more weekly newspapers and magazines than perhaps ever before in our history while overall readership of books appears to be at an all-time high.

Forget the dire forecasts of a post-industrial age or a post-literate age. What we have instead is a new age in which industry continues to play a crucial role as the foundation of our economy, the printed word still flourishes and there are ready markets for the services of hand craftsmen as well as computer experts. Instead of one economic sector replacing another in a finite economy, we have new businesses adding onto an expanding economy.

Many of the new businesses and jobs are in rapidly growing, specialized services sectors. It's been said that as a sector, health care now accounts for more jobs than steel in Hamilton.

Two-income families continue to be the norm as we carry on a successful struggle to achieve a living standard once possible with a single income. It means juggling family, social and work responsibilities. And as our lives become ever busier, we find ourselves turning more to other specialized services offered by financial planners, mortgage brokers and others.

We're still waiting for the dawn of the leisure age – and there's no point in holding our breath. Instead of ample leisure time, we're working overtime. Our society has achieved many of the luxuries of financial prosperity – except the luxury of time.

Yet, there are more jobs now and more millionaires being created now than at any other time in our history. The new age has generated an explosion of employment opportunities – although many of these jobs demand high degrees of computer literacy.

Even so, unemployment rates are falling, in part, a response to a growing tendency for people to take the entrepreneurial leap and create their own jobs.

Opened in 1993, GHTEC (Greater Hamilton Technology Enterprise Centre) has worked as an effective incubator for new technology-based businesses. Operated by the BAC (Business Advisory Centre), GHTEC, within its first few years of operation, had already helped 18 tenant firms create 128 technology jobs.

Together, these 18 firms generated $20 million in annual sales – with half of this amount going to export markets.

During the same timespan, over 600 business were started by the BAC's Entrepreneurial Program clients, who in turn created another 860 jobs.

The Michael G. DeGroote School of Business at McMaster University is another leading source of future business leaders and entrepreneurs. And they're heading into a promising future.

Offering a credible and encouraging forecast, the Toronto Dominion Bank is predicting one million jobs will be created from 1997 to the year 2000. The TD expects that 400,000 jobs will have been created in 1997 with another 300,000 new jobs to come in both 1998 and 1999.

Canada is already the fastest-growing nation of all of the G7 industrialized countries and the TD forecasts our economy will expand at an after-inflation rate of 3.7 per cent in 1997, 3.5 per cent in 1998 and 2.8 per cent in 1999, compared with a growth rate of 1.7 per cent in 1996.

The Bank of Canada also asserts that our country is in better financial shape now than it has been in many years and is well positioned to prosper in an integrated world economy.

And unemployment rates are expected to continue falling.

Our own robust, diversified, Hamilton-centred economic region can again be expected to outperform the country with higher growth levels and the lowest – or among the lowest – unemployment rates in Canada.

A study released back in October, 1997, by accounting and professional services firm KPMG, found Canada's business costs are much lower than those in the U.S. And it ranked Hamilton sixth of 17 major Canadian cities as a great place to do business.

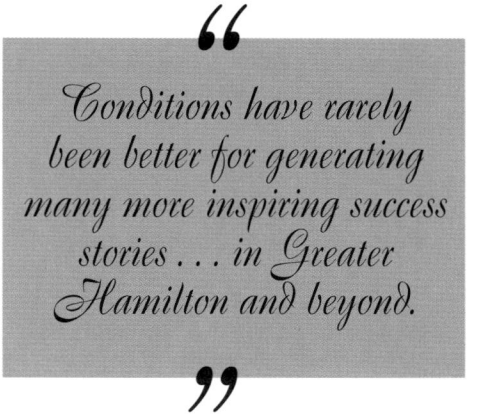

Conditions have rarely been better for generating many more inspiring success stories . . . in Greater Hamilton and beyond.

> "Conditions have rarely been better for generating many more inspiring success stories . . . in Greater Hamilton and beyond."

# Index

## A

AIC Mutual Funds, 54
Alcan Alloys, Guelph, 34
Allen, Veronica, 97
Alliance group, 66
Allwaste, 34, 35
Ambitious City, 80
American Foundries Society, 36
American Midwest, 36
Ancaster News, 76
Angrove, Norm, 102
Antel Optronics, 124
Aquafest, 42
argon laser dentistry, 94, 95
Art Gallery of Hamilton, 25
As, Czechoslovakia, 116
Atlas Specialty Steels, 12
Audit Bureau of Circulation, 76

## B

B&V Construction, 116
Baby Boomers, 48
Bailey Brazeau, Nancy, 15
Bank of Canada, 125
Bank of Montreal, 101
Barrientos, Dr. Nona, 92
Bart, Chris, 68
Bass, Paul, 92
Battaglia, Tony, 38, 39
Bay Area Implementation Team, 44
Baylor College of Dentistry, 94
BCL Magnetics, 124
Bell & Mackenzie, 44
Bell Canada, 82, 104
Belliveau, Robert, 104, 106
Beneficial Finance, 52
Berkshire Hathaway, 55
Berkshire Group, 49, 54-55, 128
Birchside Builders, 111, 116-117, 128
Biz Magazine, 76
Blockbuster Video, 65
Bo-Teek Farms, 16
Boom, Bust & Echo, 48
Boril, Otto, 116
Brabant chain, 76
Brandt, Lisa, 80
BRaSH Publishing Inc., 2, 4, 86
Brock University, 12
Bronfman, Charles, 62
Brookfield, Jeff, 44
Brown Boggs, 86
Browning, Wendy, 84
Buchanan, Isaac, 26
Buffett, Warren, 54
Burlington Environmental, 34
Burlington Gazette, 86
Business Advisory Centre, 59, 60, 128
Business Executive, 76, 128

## C

Cambridge Group, 86
Campbell, Charlie, 112
Canada Coach Lines, 94
Canada Investment Plan, 22
Canada Iron, 36
CMHC, 110
Canada's Heartland Harbour, 44
Canada-U.S. BorderNet Alliance, 26
Canadian Cancer Society, 98
Canadian Foundry Association, 36
Canadian Gross National Product, 30
Canadian Pacific, 64
Canadian Press (CP), 78, 100
CRTC, 104

Canadian Tire, 82
Canadian wine industry, 16
CanAmera Foods, 44
Candy, John, 86
Canon North America, 72
Carey, William, 78
CARSTAR, 91, 102-103, 128
Carter, Jimmy, 62
Case Western Reserve University, 94
Case, James, 84
Casino Niagara, 12
Catalano, Nick, 22, 23
CBC Television, 78, 82
CFL Hamilton Tiger-Cats, 65, 80, 100
CHAM 820 country music radio, 76
Chatelaine magazine, 78
Chinese Chamber of Commerce, 26
CHML Radio, 76, 77, 80-81, 128
CHML's Christmas Tree of Hope, 80
Chong, Tommy, 100
CJXY FM, Classic Rock Y95, 80
CKDS FM, 80
CKOC, Oldies 1150 Radio, 74, 76, 77
Clark, Valerie, 84
Cleave, Amy, 99
Cleave, Paul, 98-99
Coca Cola, 70
Collins, Pat, 76, 78
Comtek Advanced Structures, 58
Conrath, David, 68
Conversion Resources Inc., 34
Cooke, Catherine, 91, 94, 96-97, 128
Cooke, Kevin, 91, 94-95, 97, 128
Cooke, Frank Sr., 94
Cooke, Frank Jr., 94
Cooke, Richard, 94
Cooke, Terry, 5, 94
Cootes Paradise, 9
Copley Group, 86
Cowling, Dorie, 80
Coyne, Andrew, 78
Coyote Vision Group, 102
Craig, Al, 80
Cranston, Toller, 15
CRS Robotics, 124

## D

Dairy Queen, 70
Dana Canada Inc., 12
David Gruggen Photography, 128
Davie, Alistair, 58
Davie, Donovan, 4
Davie, Michael B., 4, 9, 48, 49, 61, 86
Davie, Pearl, 30
Davie, Philippa, 4, 48, 49, 86
Davie, Ryan, 4
Davie, Sarah, 4, 62
Davis, Geena, 100
De Feo Auto Service, 44
Deere, John Ltd., 12
DeGroote, Gary, 64
DeGroote, Joni, 64
DeGroote, Michael G., 9, 60-69
DeGroote Bus. School, 61, 64, 68-69
DeGroote, Michael Jr., 64
DeGroote, Tim, 64
Desperadoes taverns, 98
Despond, Frank, 52, 53
Dofasco, 9, 22, 30, 42, 58, 86, 124
Doherty, Jake, 20
Dominion Castings, 36
Dominion of Canada Insurance, 120
Dominion Pattern, 36-37, 124, 128
Doucette, Laura, 94
Dundas Star-Journal, 76
Dundas, 5, 64, 99

DuPont Canada, 68
Durritt, Ray, 86
Dynamic and Proto Circuits, 124

## E

Earle, Peter, 30
Eastport ship viewing parkette, 44
Elco Home Fashions, 86
Elliot Lake, 62
Ellis, Bryan, 82, 83
England, 42, 72
Entrepreneur of the Year, 1995, 101
Enviro-Ganics Ecological Systems, 13
Ernst & Young, 86
Estok, Mary, 114
Estrabillo, Roland, 91, 92-93, 128
Estrabillo, Maria, 92
Everson, Neil, 30, 32, 48, 90, 110

## F

Factor Forms Niagara Ltd., 12
Family Fitness, 91, 100-101, 128
Fatjo, Thomas, 65
Federal Express Canada, 38
Firestone, 70
First United Church, 77
Flaherty, Joe, 86
Flamborough News, 76
Fleet Industries Ltd., 13
Foot, David, 48
Forbes Magazine, 54, 62
Fracassi, Allen, 30, 34-35, 120
Fracassi, Enzo, 34
Fracassi, Philip, 30, 34-35, 120
Freeman, Rob, 104, 105, 106
Fursman, Frank, 84

## G

G7 industrialized countries, 125
G7 Summit, 86
Gamble, Nancy, 84
General Electric, 36
General Motors of Canada, 12, 15, 36
Genesco, Sunni, 77
Gennum Inc., 58, 124
George Sinclair Const., 112-115, 128
Gherson, Giles, 78
Giardini, Paul, 120-121
Giardini, Rita, 120
Global Television, 82
Globe & Mail, 26, 76
Gonzales, Dr. Alex, 92
Goodale, Ralph, 16
Gore Mutual Insurance, 120
Gore Park, 21
Great Lakes, 30, 32, 42, 44
GHTEC, 23, 58, 59, 125
Green, Roy, 80
Gruggen, Christopher, 86
Gruggen, David, 4, 77, 86-88
Gruggen, Dorothy, 86
Grupe, Bernd, 90
Gulf Canada Resources, 64
GWD Investments, 64

## H

Halifax Insurance Co., 120
Hamilton Chamber, 26-27, 128
Hamilton Better Business Bureau, 23
Hamilton CMA, 20, 110
Hamilton Comm. Credit Union, 30
Hamilton Construction, 110, 128
Hamilton Convention Centre, 25

Hamilton Harbour Comm., 44-45
Hamilton International Airport, 5, 32, 38-41, 70, 71, 128
Hamilton Magazine, 76, 86
Hamilton Mountain News, 76
Hamilton Sesquicentennial, 26, 80
Hamilton Spectator, 4, 48, 65, 74, 76, 77, 78-79, 86, 101, 104, 124, 128
Hamilton Street Railway (HSR), 94
Hamilton: It's Happening, 4, 5, 86
Hamilton-Wentworth Economic Development, 22, 86, 90, 110, 128
Harbour West Marina Complex, 44
Hardy, John, 80
Hartwick, Darryl, 80
Hayes, Matt, 77
Heirwegh, Sandie, 59, 60
Hennessy, Bob, 44
Hewitt, Ron, 98
Hillfield-Strathallan College, 64
Hodgson, Bob, 68
Holbrook, Elizabeth, 14, 15, 26
Hooper, Bob, 80, 81
Horton, Tim, 70
Howard, Erin, 15, 72-73
Howard, John, residence, 56
Howard, John, 15, 16-17, 60, 72-73
Huizenga, Wayne, 65, 66
Human Kinetics, 96
Hyundai Space and Aircraft Co., 13

## I

I-COR, Interlake Corridor, 20
I.W. & S. Ferrous, 34
Industry Canada, 22
Information Age, 90
Intermetco Inc., 34
International Alliance, 66
International Harvester, 36, 44
International Wendy's, 70
Intsel Southwest Partnership, 34
Investors Group, 54
Iqbal, Asim, 100, 101
ISO 9001, 36
Istona, Mildred, 78

## J

Jackson, Lloyd D. Square, 25
Jahnke, Dieter, 15, 16, 17, 72
Jankevicius, Roman, 118
Jeffries, Larry, 102
Jetport, 38, 70, 71
Jonathon's Flooring, 120
Joyce, Ron, 38, 61, 70-71
Juno Awards, 100

## K

K-Lite 102.9 FM, 77
Kachmarsky, Marie, 110
Kay, Gene, 100, 101
Kinsella, W. P., 38
Kirkby, Lee, 23, 30, 32, 48, 58, 60, 90, 124
KPMG, 125, 128
Kuhn, Lynda, 34, 35

## L

LIUNA, 38
Laidlaw Inc., 22, 38, 62
Laidlaw, Robert, 62
Lake Erie, 12, 20
Lake Ontario, 9, 12, 15, 20, 72
Lakeport Brewing, 86

# Index

Langton Contracting Co. Ltd., 62
LaPointe, Kirk, 78, 79
Lax industrial lands, 44
Lazarowich, Jon, 84
Leander Boat Club, 44
Lee-Chin, Michael, 54
Lees, George, 80
Leppert Business Equipment, 124
Levy, Eugene, 86
Liebersbach, Ruth, 102
Linear Technology, 58
London Telecom, 91, 104-107, 128
Luntz Corp., 34
Luzzi, Don, 80

## M

Macdonald, Jim, 82, 83
Maclean's magazine, 68
Malatesta, Sam, 102
Manor Cleaners, 120
Maple Leaf Broadcasting, 77
Marr, Gordon, 52, 53
Martin, Andrea, 86
Mazza, Paul, 15, 16, 17, 72
McGuire, Reg, 82
McKeil Marine, 33, 42-43, 44, 128
McKeil, Blair, 42, 43
McKeil, Doug, 42
McKeil, Evans, 42
McKeil, Florence, 42
McKeil, Garth, 42
McKeil, William, 42
McKeown, Casey, 80
McMaster University, 86, 125, 128
McNamara Marine Co., 42
Medcalf Realty, 111, 118-119, 128
Medcalf, Chris, 111, 118, 119
Medcalf, Donna, 118
Medcalf, Harvey, 118, 119
Mercanti, Anthony, 102
Mercanti, Guerino, 102
Mercanti, Nardino, 102
Mercanti, Remo, 102
Mercanti, Sam, 102, 103
Mercanti, Tony, 102
Metropolitan Hamilton Real Estate Board, 110, 118, 128
Micro Aide, 90, 128
Midence, Dr. Carlana, 92
Miller, Cathy, 84
MINT Research Centre, 68
Multiple Listing Service, 110, 118
Mohawk College, 4, 23, 26, 50, 76, 86
Money Concepts, Stoney Creek, 50
Montreal Trust, 52
Morrow, Mayor Robert, M., 5
Mortgage Advantage, 49, 52-53, 128
Mortgage Financial Corp., 52
Mr. Mugs Coffee, 91, 98-99, 128
Muscle & Fitness magazine, 100
Mutual Life, 52

## N

NADbank '97, 76
National Accounts Program, 34
National Bank of Canada, 52
NBR Realty, 94
New World Culinary Centre, 16
New York State, 12
Newfoundland, Hibernia, 42
Niagara Bench, 112
Niagara College, 4, 12, 13
Niagara Economic and Tourism Corporation, 12, 128
Niagara Escarpment Commission, 16

Niagara Falls Review, 12, 76
Niagara Falls City Centre, 12
Niagara Falls, 2, 8, 9, 10, 20, 39, 72
Niagara Land Co., 15, 16-17, 72, 128
Niagara, 12, 15, 20, 23, 76, 82, 110
Niagara River, 9, 12
Niagara wine industry, 16, 72
Niagara-on-the-Lake, 14, 15
Nortel, 68
Nortru, 34
Nova Analytical Systems, 86

## O

O'Hara, Catherine, 86
OE Canada, 72
Office Equipment Hamilton, 72
Okanogan Valley, 12
Ontario Auto Collision, 102-103, 128
Ontario Business Journal, 104
Ontario Hostelry Institute, 70
Ontario Legislature, 112
Ontario Ministry of Natural Resources, 16
Ontario Ministry of Transportation, 82
Ontario Special Olympics, 101
Ontario Wine Route, 16
ONtv, 76, 82-83, 86, 128
Orlick Industries, 86
Otis Elevator, 36, 44

## P

Pacific Northwest, 34
Pacific Rim, 16, 72
Paul Wright Memorial Award, 112
Paul's Restorations, 111, 120-121, 128
Peace, Dan, 30, 36, 37
Peace, Gordon, 30, 36
Peace, Harold V., 36
Pearson International Airport, 38
Pelham Herald, 76
Peters, Tom, 76
Peters, Wendy, 76
Philip Services, 22, 30, 34-35, 128
Philip Utilities, 34
Phoenix newspaper, 4, 76, 86
Picone, Mark, 16
Pieczonka, Dr. Wally, 58
Port of Hamilton, 32
Port Weller Dry Docks, 15, 42
Prague Spring of 1968, 116
Procter & Gamble, 30, 86
Puckering, Cathy, 102
Puder, Cathy, 52-53
Puder, Rainer, 48, 49, 52-53
Pugwash, Nova Scotia, 42
Purolator Courier, 38

## Q

Quality Management Institute, 36
Quantum, 68
Queen Elizabeth Way, 12, 32
Queen's Landing Hotel, 15
Queen's Park, 4
Queen's Quay West, 13

## R

Ramada Parkway Inn, 15
Rapid Prototyping, 36
Ready-Mix, 38
Real Estate News, 76
Redhill Freeway, 32
Renaissance, 20, 23, 128
Republic Environmental, 65, 66

Republic Industries Inc., 65, 66
Richler, Mordecai, 78
Rockcliffe Research, 34
Rose, Fred, 44
Royal Bank, 68
Royal Canadian Air Force, 112
Royal Canadian Navy, 42, 70
Royal Connaught hotel, 24, 25, 78
Royal Hamilton Yacht Club, 44
Royal Insurance Co., 120
Royal Trust, 52
Ruberto, Bruno, 4, 86

## S

S&B Food Equipment, 44
Santucci, Jerry, 49, 54-55, 128
Scaletta, Sandra, 84
Schinkel, Bob, 110
Scouts Canada, 4th Ancaster, 30
Second City TV, 86
Second World War, 26, 42, 62, 118
Serv-Tech, 34, 35
Shaker Cruise Lines, 13
Shaw Cafe & Wine Bar, 14
Shaw, George Bernard (statue) 14, 15
Sheraton Hamilton Hotel, 25, 91
Sherwin, Bob, 77
Shiffer, Claudia, 100
Si Wai Lai, 15
Sinclair Cut Stone, 112
Sinclair, Bill, 112, 114, 115
Sinclair, Bud, 111, 112-115
Sinclair, George, 112, 114
Skylon Tower, 12
Slack, Herb, 76
Slater Steel, 36
Sleightholm, Sherry, 4
Smart, Phil, 68
Smart, Rich, 68
Smiley, Robert, 78
Smith, Adam, 20
Soble, Ken, 80, 82
Southam Inc., 76, 78
Southam News, 78
Southam, William, 78
Spragge, Dave, 80
St. Catharines Standard, 12, 76
St. Catharines, 12, 15, 110
St. Lawrence Seaway, 32, 42
St. Mary's University, 64
Statistics Canada, 30
Stelco Hilton Works, 32, 33
Stelco Inc., 9, 22, 30, 50, 58, 94, 124
Stirling Print-All, 77, 84-85, 128
Stirling, Bill, 84
Stirling, Bob, 84, 85
Stirling, Mary, 84
Stonehouse, Mark, 100
Stoney Creek News, 76
Sturrup, Bill, 80
Success Stories, 4, 5, 9, 48, 65, 76, 86
Sun Syndicate, 125
Swenor, Bob, 26
Symix Software Inc., 68

## T

Talk 640, 80
TDL Group, 70, 128
The Co-operators Insurance Co., 120
Thomas, Dave, 86
Thompson, Dan, 102
Thomson, Kenneth, 62
Tiara restaurant, 15
Tim Horton Children's Foundation, 70
Toronto Dominion Bank, 52, 125

Toronto Dominion Bank forecast, 125
Toronto Star, 76
Toronto Stock Exchange index, 78
Toronto Sun, 76, 125
Toronto Telegram, 125
Tradeport International, 38, 39, 128
TRW - Canada Ltd., 12

## U

U.S. Surgeon General's Report, 100
United Parcel Service, 32, 38
United States, 12, 26, 36, 94
United States, rustbelt regions, 30
University of Guelph, 96
University of Toronto, 92
USAir, 38

## V

Vacca & Assoc., 48, 49, 50-51, 128
Vacca, Armando, David, 48, 49, 50-51
Vacca, Pasqualino, 50
Vancouver Airport Authority, 38
Vineland Estates, 15-16, 60, 72, 128
Vineland, 15, 16
VQA (Vintners Quality Alliance), 12
Vision 2020, 22
Visual Applications Software Inc., 68
Voice Recovery Services, 15
Votruba, Sandy, 116
Votruba, Vaclav, 116
Votruba, Wes, 116, 117

## W

Wall Street, 66
Wallace, Ron, 58, 59
Warrenton Resources Inc., 34
Waste Management Corp., 65
Wastewater Technology Centre, 34
Watson, Mike, 100, 101
Waxman Resources, 34
Waxman, Robert, 34
Weber, Ron, 90
Weis, Hermann, 15, 16, 17, 72
Weisz, Jim, 106
Welland Canal, 31, 32, 44
Welland Tribune, 4, 12, 76
Wescam Inc., 86, 124
Westbury Bermuda, 65
Westbury International, 64
Western University, 54
Westinghouse Canada, 36, 58
Weston, Galen, 62
Westpark Developments Inc., 38
Whyte, Patrick, 58
WIC, 82, 83
Wilkie, Ian, 84
Wilkie, Ron, 84
WinTel Communications Inc., 106
Winter Festival of Lights, 12
Wood, Colin, 106

## X

Xerox, 72

## Y

Young Drivers of Canada, 82
YVR Airport Services, 38

## Z

Zenon, 124
Zurich Insurance Co., 120

## Directory

This directory is provided as a special feature intended to assist researchers and others who may be interested in obtaining further information from some of the companies, individuals and organizations cited in this book.

*Birchside Builders Inc.*
(905) 385-1288

*The Business Executive*
(905) 845-8300

*CARSTAR Automotive Canada*
*(Ontario Auto Collision)*
(905) 388-2264

*CHML 900 / Y95 Radio*
(905) 521-9900

*Dr. Kevin Cooke*
(905) 388-1977

*Dr. Catherine Cooke*
(905) 574-3274

*Michael G. DeGroote School of Business*
(905) 525-9140 ext. 27634

*Dominion Pattern Works*
(905) 544-2505

*Dr. Roland Estrabillo, Dentist*
(905) 387-2600

*International Family Fitness Centres*
*and The One Club for Women*
(905) 578-9800

*David Gruggen Photography*
(905) 522-1031

*Hamilton Construction Association*
(905) 522-5220

*Hamilton & District Chamber of Commerce*
(905) 522-1151

*Hamilton-Halton Home Builders' Association*
(905) 575-3344

*Hamilton-Wentworth Economic*
*Development Department*
(905) 546-4447

*Hamilton International Airport and*
*Tradeport International*
(905) 679-4151

*The Hamilton Spectator*
(905) 526-3333

*Ron Joyce / TDL Group*
*(Tim Donut Co., Tim Hortons Donuts)*
(905) 845-9096

*KPMG*
(905) 523-8200

*London Telecom*
(905) 570-8700

*McKeil Marine*
(905) 528-4780

*Medcalf Realty Ltd.*
(905) 547-7303

*Metropolitan Hamilton*
*Real Estate Board*
(905) 529-8101

*Micro Aide Computers*
(905) 648-0750

*Mr. Mugs Coffee & Donuts*
(519) 752-9890

*Mortgage Advantage Corporation Inc.*
(905) 318-6700

*Niagara Economic*
*and Tourism Corporation*
(905) 685-1308

*Niagara Land Company,*
*Vineland Estates, John Howard*
(905) 562-7088

*ONtv*
(905) 522-1101

*Renaissance*
(905) 546-2560

*Paul's Restorations*
(905) 388-7285

*Philip Services Corp.*
(905) 521-1600

*Jerry Santucci,*
*Berkshire Investment Group*
(905) 319-9000

*George Sinclair Construction Inc.*
(905) 561-9320

*Stirling Print-All*
(905) 525-5467

*A.D. Vacca & Associates*
*Financial Planning Group*
(905) 549-7526

## Patrons

June and Ron Cleave

Country Chocolates, Cambridge

Davey International - Georgiana Yao

Cameron Davie

Gay & Randy Davie

Kirby Davie

Pearl & Robert Davie

De Feo's Auto Service Limited

Aldo DeSantis Realty Inc.

Emerald Limousine Service

Fluke Transport Ltd.

Gailmount Men's Hairstyling

Pat & Tony Cosoleto

La Costa Restaurant

Diane & Eugene Martinello

Dr. Sean P. McDonough, Dentist

Ralph Mete General Contracting

Micro Aide Computers

Mohawk College of
Applied Arts & Technology

Royal Connaught
Howard Johnson Plaza Hotel

Frank Ruberto

Maria & Tony Ruberto

Rosa & Agostino Ruberto

Theresa Ruberto

Schinkel Real Estate Appraisals

Shoppers Drug Mart Stoney Creek
Matthew J. Neskar, Manager

Stelco Hilton Works

Dr. Iwona Tarasiewicz

Toronto Dominion Bank,
Aberdeen & Dundurn Branch

Lou Triantafillou

Venetian Jewellers Ltd.

Laura & Frank Wysocki